Breaking Free

Breaking Free

How I Escaped Polygamy, the FLDS Cult,

and My Father, Warren Jeffs

Rachel Jeffs

HARPER

An Imprint of HarperCollins*Publishers*

This book is an account of my experiences in the FLDS, told to the best of my ability and recollection. Some names have been changed to protect the privacy of certain individuals.

FIRST EDITION

All photos courtesy of the author

Designed by Leah Carlson-Stanisic

Library of Congress Cataloging-in-Publication Data has been applied for.

ISBN 978-0-06-267053-3

23 24 25 26 27 LBC 8 7 6 5 4

I dedicate this book to my children, Ember, Majasa, Rulon, Lavinder, and Nathaniel, and to anyone and everyone who has had difficult experiences in their lives. You can be strong and fulfill your dreams.

Contents

PART THREE

Author's Note

I am not a victim, and I do not want anyone's sympathy. I wrote this book to help others who have suffered from similar experiences, whether in the FLDS church, or in thrall to some other circumstance beyond their control. I want people to know that it is possible not only to overcome their trials but also to use those difficult experiences to help others. No matter where you came from or what you've been through, we are all in this together.

Breaking Free

One week into my marriage, I was a wreck. I couldn't eat. My skin felt prickly, like I was being poked all over by a thousand invisible needles. This was a new experience for me, being a plural wife, but it was also new for my sister wives to have me there. They hadn't asked for another woman to join their ranks, and I was starting to get the message that they weren't exactly pleased I had been added to the family, or that I was sharing our husband's bed. They didn't know that I was just sleeping in it, and not very well at that. On nights when one of the other ladies shared our husband's bed, I slept on the couch in the living room. I didn't have a room of my own.

Four weeks into my marriage, I was still getting acclimated. I didn't love my husband, Rich, yet, but I had started to like him. I enjoyed his company, anyway.

One afternoon, I was helping him with some yard work.

"Rachel, would you please go get my pruning shears?" Rich said. "They should be in the closet in my room."

I put down my rake and went into the house. In his bedroom, there was a beautiful bouquet of roses on the desk, with a small balloon attached that read "I love you." There was also a little note: "Dear Rachel, happy 4 week anniversary, I love you, Rich."

I'd cried a lot since the wedding, but the tears that fell now felt different. I was grateful that Rich wasn't there to see my reaction, because I cared what he thought about me. I couldn't have explained my feelings, because I didn't understand them myself. I found the shears and went back outside.

"Thanks," I said, as I handed the shears to him.

Rich smiled at me. "I wanted to do something for you."

"I like it," I said, and meant it.

It was a full two months after our wedding before I finally summoned up the nerve to ask Rich for a baby. I had been way too frightened to be intimate with a man I'd met only one day before he became my husband. I was still a little scared, but he had a big grin on his face when I said it.

"Do you know how to make a baby, Rachel?" Rich said, with genuine concern in his voice. The church separated boys and girls before puberty hit. At home and at school, we were kept apart. Crushes weren't allowed. Dating wasn't even an idea. Marriage was our introduction to intimate relationships.

Nonetheless, I said, "Yes."

Rich's eyes opened wide, and he tilted his head to the side like a dog that's just heard an unfamiliar sound. "Really? How do you know?"

"I just do," I said, turning my face away from him. I couldn't look him in the eyes.

That night I joined him in his room. Rich undressed himself, then undressed me as I lay on the bed. "Do you want to see?" he said, hovering over me.

"No!" I squeezed my eyes shut.

"My other ladies wanted to see."

"I don't. I really don't."

Over the next nights, I started to relax, and being with my new husband got easier. I soon learned that I was pregnant. When I was about four months along, Rich said, "How did you know about sex before we were married?"

Rich was my husband, and now the father of my unborn child. I had kept this secret for so many years, I hardly knew how to answer him. And then, just like that, I did.

"Father taught me."

Part One

1

You Could Drive a Car Through My Family Tree

There is only one man on the earth at a time that can receive direct revelation from God, and it is God's Prophet.

—WARREN S. JEFFS

Hildale, Utah, November 25, 1986

"Rachel, Becky, come here."

Father was standing next to the Prophet's casket at the front of the meeting house. The Prophet was Leroy Johnson, the leader of the Fundamentalist Church of Latter-Day Saints (FLDS) and the only man on earth worthy of receiving the word of God, but we knew him as Uncle Roy.

My sister Becky and I walked over to the casket. Our father was Warren Jeffs, and he was the principal of our church school. Father took one of our little hands in each of his, and we held on tight. I had just turned three years old, and Becky was two months younger than me. Our mothers, Father's first two wives, were sisters, and had been pregnant with Becky and me at the same time.

"Can we get these girls a stool so they can see?" Father asked one of Uncle Roy's wives standing in line, waiting to pay their respects to Uncle Roy. I could hear people crying.

A lady with gray hair brought over a small yellow stool and placed it in front of the casket. Father helped me up onto it first. I had never seen a dead person before. I looked inside the coffin, curious and frightened, at the withered, pale figure lying there. He didn't look at all like the bald man with the benevolent smile I'd only seen in pictures. He was so very old, and his face looked white and fake. He had been sick for a long time.

I hadn't met Uncle Roy while he was alive, but I knew he had been the leader of the church since before my father was born.

Father leaned into me, put his mouth next to my ear, and quietly said, "Uncle Roy was the greatest man on earth. Rachel, I want you to never forget what a privilege it is that you have seen the Prophet."

The most important rule in the FLDS religion is this: Never question the Prophet. Even after Uncle Roy's death, Father continued to read his sermons to us every day at 6:00 a.m. before breakfast—before we did anything else at all, in fact. These readings were considered vital to our spiritual growth.

Uncle Roy's teachings were very specific. People in our church should conduct themselves with humility and obedience—to the church, to our parents, to our husbands. Women had to wear long dresses, with sleeves to their wrists and skirts to their ankles. Boys should not so much as touch a girl's arm before marriage. The Prophet determined who and when a person should marry.

With Uncle Roy's passing, my paternal grandfather, Rulon T. Jeffs, assumed the mantle of Prophet of the FLDS. While Grandfather Rulon was still alive, Father preached to us about the Prophet from the stand at the meeting house and from his living room chair almost every day. "God and the Prophet do right," Father said.

Being the descendant of a Prophet made you something like royalty in the FLDS. I, and some of my siblings, had Prophet blood on both sides of the family.

Uncle Roy had been the Prophet since 1949, three years before declaring our church a completely separate entity from the Church of the Latter-Day Saints in Salt Lake City (commonly called the Mormon Church). Before that schism, our church had considered itself a subsidiary of the main church in Salt Lake, but in truth, Uncle Roy's declaration was kind of a formality; our people had already been excommunicated from the traditional LDS Church back in 1935 for refusing to give up polygamy.

In those days, the Prophet had been John Y. Barlow, whose older brother, Ianthus Barlow, was my maternal great-grandfather. Ianthus left the church when his brother became the Prophet because he didn't want to follow his younger brother, but Ianthus continued to practice and teach his family to live polygamy.

More than four decades later, in 1978, Ianthus's son, Isaac Barlow—my mother's father—rejoined the church with his family. By then, Uncle Roy was the Prophet. The Barlows stayed for only a few years, but it was long enough for Isaac's daughter Annette, and three years later his daughter Barbara, to marry a young schoolteacher named Warren Jeffs. Both girls were seventeen years old at the time of their weddings.

I was born in Salt Lake City in 1983, the oldest child of Father's second wife, Barbara Barlow. That made me the first child born into his polygamous family, his first plural child. My sister Becky, who was summoned to Uncle Roy's casket with me, was born to Barbara's older sister, Annette, technically making Becky my cousin as well as my sister, although we never thought of it that way. It wasn't uncommon for sisters to marry the same man. It was right after my mother's wedding to Father that her family, the Barlows, left the church again. They objected to my mother's not being allowed to choose her husband, but Uncle Roy had told my mother to marry my father, and that was that. The Barlows took all of their other children with them when they left, leaving Annette and Barbara to their fate within the church.

According to the FLDS church, leaving is the most wicked thing you can do, and Father taught his young wives that they were so very blessed to have married him because the Barlow family would all be down in hell, and only the two of them were good enough to escape damnation. I don't know if this was why Mother Annette and Mother Barbara weren't affectionate with their children. I knew my mother loved me, but she was hard to get close to, and she didn't talk very much. She would never hug one of her children for no reason; it just wasn't her way. Mother Annette was the same with Becky and her other children. Father sometimes said it was up to him to be both mother and father to us, as though it was his role to be close to the children. Yet the mothers who came later, who came from families in the church, did not withhold their affection from their children.

This is how I grew up in Sandy, Utah, a suburb of Salt Lake City, knowing that we were different from everyone else. Our families were large, we dressed modestly, our hair had to be braided a certain way. We belonged to a church the outside world didn't seem to understand.

"It's good to be different," Father would often say to us children. "If we were like everyone else in the world, we would be very wicked like they are."

"That is why you children are so special," he said, "because you are privileged to know the Prophet, the greatest man in the world. He gives us teachings straight from the Heavenly Father."

As principal of our private church school, Alta Academy, Father had full control of what we learned. Every morning at the beginning of the school day, there was morning class, held in the meeting room, which all of the students attended together. Father taught us about the dress code, about keeping our bodies covered, and that boys must not touch girls and vice versa. Afterward we all lined up and went off to our various academic classes. The boys and girls shared classes through fifth grade, and then the boys and girls were separated, and the girls no longer had any communication or social life with the boys.

None of the teachers at the church school had gone to college, including Father, but Father was a very good teacher all the same. He'd taught himself how to program computers, and he could explain math all the way through trigonometry. We were also taught reading, science, history, and English up through eighth grade.

In addition, we were schooled in the history of the Mormon Church (at least as the FLDS saw it). We learned that Joseph Smith had been a chosen Prophet of the Lord, and that Mormons had been persecuted and driven from their land in the nineteenth century. We were taught that the world was always, and would always be, against us. Our only protection was to obey the Prophet. And if we ever left the church, we would be damned, and of all of hell's angels we would be the most miserable. If we were good and stayed sweet, then we would be blessed.

We lived in a lovely area at the mouth of Little Cottonwood Canyon, about six miles east of downtown Sandy, and Father often took us hiking up the mountain across the street. Home was an unremarkable brick house built in the 1970s, but there were eight bedrooms, one for each mother, and the children shared with the siblings closest to our own age, which were usually half siblings. Boys and girls not only didn't share rooms but were forbidden to enter one another's rooms—ever.

Becky and I were allowed to watch a couple of kids' movies when we were little—I remember *Bambi* and *Cinderella*—on a VCR in our grandmother's bedroom. We were also allowed a few children's books and schoolbooks, from which we learned to read. Books from the outside world—"gentile" books—were monitored very closely. Romance titles, especially, were forbidden; it was wicked to even think about a boy, let alone like one.

We had very little money—Father didn't earn much of a salary as the principal of our church school. Most of the family's income was generated by Mother Barbara, who did commercial sewing out of the house. We had several large industrial sewing machines in the family room. Sometimes we children would help Mother clip threads and turn her finished products right side out. But with so many of us to support, there was still never enough. Father refused to live off the government, so we did not have food stamps, Medicaid, or any of the other kinds of assistance that other FLDS families relied on when they needed to.

As a result, all of our furniture and bedding came from secondhand stores. Nothing matched. There was ugly pea-green carpeting throughout the house, and our hideous secondhand couches were embarrassing. I loved it when every once in a while we'd get something new from Kmart or some other discount store. I dreamed of having a beautiful home with matching couches in the living room, coordinating rugs and towels in the bathroom, and my own bedroom where the furniture and décor harmonized.

There were several bathrooms, but there was one no one used unless you were in danger of wetting yourself. That one was off the mudroom by the kitchen—we called it the mud bathroom. It was always messy, and the toilet seat was always freezing. Since no one liked to use it, it was a good place to hide and read a "gentile" book if you could get your hands on one.

Every morning Father drew up a list of chores for us, and no one was left out. He would put a mother and certain children on kitchen duty to prepare the meals and clean up, another mother and several children on house cleaning. A mother and older children were tasked with tending the younger children.

Every day, one mother and one of us girls was assigned to laundry duty, and it took all day. Laundry was an enormous chore, and I hated it when it was my turn. There were no laundry hampers, so there were always great piles of children's clothes on the floor. The entire family's laundry pile looked like a mountain to me, and it had to be sorted and folded into each person's individual basket. One mother overheard me complain about having to do all that folding and yelled down to the basement to me, "You can't come upstairs until it's done!" Complaining was considered a sin, so my punishment could actually have been more severe.

We had a nice-size kitchen, but mostly empty cupboards. It seemed like there was never enough food to eat, and what there was, we children thought was pretty yucky. There were years when we didn't eat much milk or meat, and we never had sugar or any kind of processed cereal or candy. The mothers would get buckets of raw honey when they could afford it. Mostly we subsisted on homemade whole-wheat brick bread, mush, beans, veggies in the summer when we grew them, and a lot of brown rice.

In other ways, our childhood wasn't so different from what children outside the church experienced, except we had a bigger family than most. I was the third of seven girls in a row before Father's first sons were born. My sister Becky and I were practically twins. We shared a bedroom, secrets, everything. When we were five, Father had us start violin lessons with Jennifer Wall, who was extremely talented and made the learning fun for us. (She eventually married Father.) We played with our dolls and rode bikes, and we went swimming every Thursday at our uncle Wallace's pool. Father taught us all how to swim when I was seven. He took extra time with me, teaching me all the different strokes and how to dive. Every Friday night we each had to get up in front of the family and perform a song or a play. Father took us fishing at least once every summer. When Father came home from a stressful day at work, he'd ask us children to act out plays and skits for him. Sometimes he would join in, acting out silly antics to make us laugh. He favored the girls, and spent far more special time with us doing fun things than he did with the boys.

Most of the time, our imaginations were our favorite entertainment. Using the few movies and books we'd read, we pretended for hours, making up stories and adventures to keep ourselves amused when we were not in school or doing our assigned chores. There was also a large front yard, and a small forest of trees in the backyard—we called it "the woods"—where Becky and I went to get away from everyone else and build huts or tree houses. It was our happy place.

There was also a large garden that we planted with all kinds of vegetables during the spring and summer. Each day, one of the girls would be assigned to water and weed. There was a small orchard of fruit trees—apple, plum, pear, peach, and apricot— and we often snacked on the unripe fruit. There was also a beautiful array of roses by the front porch. The bush closest to the front door was my favorite: a Peace rose, which produced large flowers of pink and yellow.

Encircling this Eden was a six-foot-tall cement wall, a defining characteristic of every house I lived in. As a child, I thought these walls were meant to keep the wicked world outside. But in time I came to realize that they were there just as much to keep us in.

2

Sins of the Father

"Rachel, Father wants to talk to you on the phone," Mother Annette said one day in the summer of 1992.

I picked up the handset. "Rachel, come over to my office," Father said.

Father had recently started singling me out for special attention, inviting me to spend time with him without the other children around. At the time, there were seven of us girls and three little boys, aged three and younger. I had no idea why he chose me above all the others. He'd take me for a drive or shopping or to eat at a restaurant, just us two, but mostly he had me spend time with him in his office. Usually I would read one of the books he had lying around, or help him clean up or do some minor task he gave me.

When I arrived that day, the light in the office was very dim. The blinds had been pulled closed, allowing only a small stream of afternoon sunlight to peek through the slats.

"Come in, Rachel." Father was sitting in the chair behind the desk. "Come closer," he said, and waved me over to him. He pulled me onto his lap. He moved his hands around underneath me and then slid me off his lap and turned me around to face him, pushing me to my knees. His pants were undone and his genitals were exposed. I gasped. I had never seen a man's parts before, only my little brothers' when I was told to change their diapers. Father had always taught us that our bodies were sacred and that it was a sin to let anyone see them uncovered.

Father took my hand and placed it on his penis. I tried to pull away, but he held my hand firmly, placing his hand over mine. He began squeezing my hand up and down.

I closed my eyes and turned away, but with his free hand he reached for my chin and turned my face back toward him. "Rachel, look. This is what a man looks like."

I was so frightened. I wanted to run. I wanted to scream. I wanted to cry my heart out. But I didn't dare do any of that. Strict obedience to our father and mothers was the second most important rule, after never questioning the Prophet. I was afraid of what Father would do to me if I didn't obey.

"Rachel, see how a man goes hard when you touch him? Don't turn away, look."

Why is he making me do this? This is wicked. Father himself teaches us so. Is Father doing this because I am eight years old? We were taught that eight was the age of accountability, when all of our sins would be on our own head.

As his breathing got faster, the feeling of shame in my heart seemed to thicken and curdle.

I walked home from his office that afternoon feeling like a true sinner. I had done a terrible thing, and I was afraid my mothers and siblings would be able to tell what had happened in Father's office. When I got to the house, I went immediately to my bedroom. I couldn't eat dinner with my family; I was overwhelmed with guilt. Finally, as my sisters came to bed and settled in to sleep, and darkness filled the bedroom, I wept silently into my pillow until I fell asleep.

The next morning and every day afterward, Father behaved as though nothing had happened.

"Girls, let's go on a hike!" Father said as he walked in the front door one warm day in July. We scrambled to find shoes and socks, since we stayed in bare feet as much as possible in summer to keep cool. Since we had to wear long dresses and long underwear, bare feet were our only relief. There was one designated sock basket for the whole family, and we'd have to dig through it trying to find a pair. That day I ended up with one blue sock and one black sock that was too big, so the heel rode up to my ankle.

When I walked out on the porch, I saw Father with some of my sisters and our dog Sunny—one of the German shepherds we had over the years—already heading toward the road to cross over to the mountain, and I ran to catch up to them. As we stood in our obvious church dresses and braids waiting for cars to pass so we could cross, the driver of a red car lay on the horn and yelled "Plygs!" out the window at us. We got that a lot, gentiles laughing and pointing at us.

The first part of the hike was an easy walk up the dirt path to the water tank. From there, the trail steepened. Father and Sunny led the way up the deer trail to the ridge. Every so often, Sunny would come back down to check on us girls. We were lagging behind, talking and laughing and getting winded. "Girls, if you want to save energy, you'll be quiet and keep a constant pace," Father said. We quieted down and continued walking.

At the top, we climbed over the ridge and down the other side of the mountain to what we called Lookout Rock. We clambered up to the top and looked out over Bell's Canyon and a beautiful stream weaving through the valley below. It was easy to forget ugly things for a moment.

"Race you down to the stream!" Father said, and took off running.

We took off after him. As I ran, the cool canyon air blew against my face; it felt like freedom.

About halfway down, Becky and I stopped at Bell's Cave, an abandoned mining cave dug into the side of the mountain.

"Do you dare go in there?" I said to Becky.

"I don't know. It's so dark," she said. "Do you?"

We tiptoed to the mouth of the cave, Becky holding the skirt of my dress, and I the sleeve of hers. We took a few careful steps in until the darkness began to crowd us.

"I don't really feel like it right now," I said, trying not to sound afraid.

"Yeah, me neither."

Then we heard a sound at the far end of the cave. I grabbed Becky's arm and we both turned around and ran.

The other girls and Father and Sunny had already reached the stream by the time we got there. "Where were you?" Father asked with a slightly furrowed brow.

"We were trying to be brave and go in the cave," I said.

"Get a drink from the stream before we head home," he said.

We cupped our hands into the ice-cold water and drank our fill. It was a treat on such a hot day.

As we headed back down the mountain toward home, Father and Sunny walked ahead; Becky and I took our sweet time. Suddenly we heard a loud screech, followed by yelling. In the distance we could see Father running toward the road in front of our house. Becky and I started running to catch up.

"Go straight to the house," Father said. "Don't come over here."

Maryanne had been walking with Father, and she helped us younger girls cross the street, but she was crying. "The lady in the car didn't see Sunny running across the road," Maryanne said. Sunny's back right leg had been ripped off during the accident. While we sat in the hall and cried, Father went to get someone to put Sunny out of his pain.

"I'm sad about Sunny, but I'm glad it wasn't one of you girls that had been run over," he said when he came back in the house.

That night after the evening meal, we had family prayer, and Father thanked Heavenly Father that we were all safe. Then he hugged us all good night and sent us to bed.

Three days later, I was on the swings with Becky when I heard Father call out, "Rachel!" from the path that led to the school. A shudder ran through me—I'd avoided being alone with him for the last week or so, since my last visit to his office. I slowly slid out of the swing and walked toward him, my eyes on the ground.

"Come clean my office for me," Father said as I approached. "Will you?"

I knew saying "I don't want to" would anger him, although that was exactly what I wanted to say. He expected my obedience.

"Yes," I said, and continued walking with him a few steps behind.

"Rachel, why aren't you walking by me?"

I knew he knew why, but I caught up to him, keeping my arms folded to avoid any contact and trying to convince myself to ignore the bad feeling I had about this.

When we reached the school, I climbed the stairs to his office behind him. He put the key in the door, which was always locked whether he was in there or not. (His sister Rachel, the principal's assistant, was the only other person who had a key.)

I decided I would clean Father's office as quickly as I could and get out of there before anything weird happened. I got the cleaners and rags out and started washing down the windows. Father took a seat on the couch while I worked. My hands were shaking as I straightened the phone and papers on his desk. I vacuumed the floor and put the chairs in their proper place by the desk, and then I was done.

"Rachel, come here."

I looked over at him. His pants were undone, and his penis was visible.

"Come here," Father said again.

Terrified, I slowly walked toward him. When I was close enough, he took my arm and pulled me onto the couch beside him. He placed my hand on his erect penis and began moving it up and down. After a few minutes of doing that, he stood me up, lifted my dress, and pulled down my underpants. He sat me on his lap, returned my hand to his penis, and put his hand between my legs and began to rub. He didn't say a word as he did these things.

Father wasn't just my father—he was the son of the Prophet, the principal of our church school, the man entrusted with the spiritual education of all the children, most especially his own.

When he was done with me, Father said, "You can go home."

The sun on my back gave me some relief as I walked back to our house.

"Rachel, come eat your dinner," Mother Annette said when I stepped inside, as though she knew I was planning to go straight to my room again. I sat down at the place that was left for me, and my mouth went dry. Dinner that night was a dish we called "cheesy business," which consisted of whipped potatoes, corn, spaghetti sauce, and cheese. I usually liked cheesy business, but it didn't look appealing to me. I forced myself to swallow each bite until I was finished so that I did not seem disobedient.

That night as I lay in bed, I tried to convince myself that Father would probably never do those weird things to me again, that he was just feeling different this last week.

But things only got worse.

That summer, Father summoned me to his office over and over again, at least two or three times a week. Each time, he was more determined to get me to touch him on my own, without his having to take my hand and make me do it. I refused. I held my hand back and looked away, while he kept saying, "Rachel, put your hand here." In the end, he would have to put my hand on him, and he would not let me leave his office until he had had his satisfaction.

One day in his office, as he sat on the couch exposing himself to me, there was a new intensity when he said yet again, "I want you to touch me." He took hold of my arm and kept saying it over and over. "Rachel, I want you to touch me." I realized he wasn't going to let me go until I obeyed, so I did.

The next day, Father took me for a ride alone to do some shopping for school.

"You didn't pass the test yesterday," Father said, as he was driving. I looked at him, confused. *What test?* "I told you to touch me to see if you wanted to, and you did it. That shows me that you have immoral thoughts and desires."

He tells me I must obey him, and now he says he was just testing me?

I didn't say a word to him, just turned my head away to look out the window and cried silently.

"Becky, let's pretend we're camping on the mountain," I said to my sister when we were playing in the yard one afternoon. "I'll be Father, and you are my wife. Melanie, Shirley, and Angela"—our little sisters—"can be our girls." I had to play Father because

I was the oldest girl playing. Besides, we didn't have any big brothers, only little ones too young to play.

Becky went to get our sisters to join us, and I started gathering up "camping things" for our adventures—an old backpack, some play dishes, a blanket. Almost every time we played pretend, we spent more time setting everything up than actually having the adventure. It didn't matter—we thought it was fun, and we stayed out all afternoon until Mother Gloria, father's third wife, called us in for dinner. I hated to go in and break the spell of a "normal" childhood.

"Rachel, do you want to come on a ride with me?" Father asked. By this time I'd had enough experience that I could sense when he had that fishy feeling about him, but I was afraid to defy him. In the past, when I had disobeyed him, he punished me or withdrew privileges from me. He might take my sisters and brothers on an outing and tell me in front of them, "Rachel, you can't come with us." My siblings assumed I had done something naughty, and they would treat me badly for it. That hurt more than what Father did, and I couldn't bear it, so I had to make a choice. To keep my family's goodwill and affection, I had to stay on Father's good side and do what he said. It was worth it to me to have my sisters' approval, even if they hadn't the slightest idea of what I was going through.

Father took me on a drive up the canyon that day, up to the top of the mountain. When he stopped the car, he said, "I need to use the bathroom. I'll have to go in the trees. You come and stand guard." He told me where to stand and walked off a little ways.

"Rachel! Rachel! Come here!" Father called out, not a minute later.

With dread anchoring my feet, I had to drag myself step by

step toward him. I stopped a yard from where he stood. He had his back turned to me, but I could tell he was uncovered.

"Rachel, come right here."

I took another tiny step, close enough that he could reach for my arm and pull me around in front of him.

"There's a bunch of mosquitoes on me right here," Father said, pointing to his genital area. "I need you to get them off me."

"No, please," I said, trying to look away.

"Yes, I need you to." He pushed my head toward his genitals. I was short enough that I didn't have to bend down very far. "Get them off."

I pulled away, but he pulled me back toward him. "Right down there, get them off."

I began to cry, but tried to angle my face away so he wouldn't see. I didn't want him to know. *Rachel, if you want to get this over with, you'll have to do what he says. Just do it and it'll be done.* I opened my eyes. My father's intimate parts were right in front of my face.

"There are no mosquitoes!" I said.

"Yes, there are."

Father wasn't going to let me go until I touched him one way or another, so I pretended to brush away the mosquitoes.

When I was ten, Father started taking me to bookstores and libraries to show me pornography. He would park me in the children's section, then go to the back of the store where the "adult" books were shelved, choose whatever he wanted to show me, and bring it back to me. To other patrons, it looked like a loving father was simply reading to his child.

"Rachel, look what men and women do together," or "Look what men and women do to themselves."

If the children's section was busy with other kids, Father would have me follow him to a different section of the store, say gardening or earth science, where there weren't any customers around, so he could explain to me how babies were made and born in great detail. "Father, I don't want to see."

"I want you to look at these pictures."

Father put his hands on either side of my head and forced me to look. I was embarrassed that other people in the store could tell I didn't want to look at what he was showing me, so I always ended up obeying him. Many times he would take me back to his office, undress himself and me, and then have us imitate, minus the actual penetration, the positions in the pictures he'd just shown me.

I rejoiced every time Father got a new wife because with each new marriage he left me alone for a few months. Father married his fourth wife, Brenda Jessop, in the spring of 1993. When he married Monica Sue Jessop, his fifth wife, in September 1995, he left me alone for six glorious months. I loved those six months of freedom, and I loved Mother Monica for keeping him occupied.

I spent a lot of time with my sisters during those months, pretending we were camping in the "woods" in our backyard.

One day I said to Becky, "Let's play like we are gentiles, and after a while we turn good. Melanie is your girl, and Shirley and Angela are my girls. Levi"—the oldest of our little brothers—"can be the preacher who convinces us to mend our ways."

We all rolled up our sleeves and leggings to expose our limbs like the gentiles. We set up our "homes" by making little huts out of branches, and we pretended our bikes were cars for transportation.

"Let's go on a vacation together," I said. We got on our bikes and rode around the house. When we got to the glass door, we got off our bikes and admired our bare arms and legs in the reflection. It didn't occur to us that anybody inside the house could see us. We hopped back on our bikes and headed back to our huts in the woods.

Two minutes later Mother Barbara came out. "Father wants you to put on your pajamas for having bare arms and legs."

"But Mother," I said, "we were about to turn good. Levi was going to teach us about the gospel."

"Do what Father says."

We went in the house and put on our pajamas. While we changed, Mother Barbara answered a phone call. "Father wants you girls to walk over to his office," she said.

"Please, no!" we said. There were lots of people at the school. It was late summer, and the teachers were getting their classrooms ready. We'd be humiliated, parading around in our pajamas in the middle of the day.

But as always, disobeying was not an option.

Father's older brother, Leroy Jeffs, was in his office when we arrived. I was embarrassed that Uncle Leroy saw us in our pajamas.

"Have a seat," Father said, motioning to the chairs in front of his desk. "I'm going to spank you because you know what you were doing was wrong. Why would you ever want to be like the gentiles? They are filthy and immoral. That is why they go naked."

Father picked up a yardstick and spanked me first, since I was the oldest, then Becky and Melanie.

"You should be grateful that you are part of the priesthood," Father said when he was done.

3

Mind Games

"Get up, girls!" Father said one morning, flipping on the light in our bedroom, and then kept walking down the hall.

"But we're so tired!" Becky said. We both fell immediately back to sleep.

Father came back a few minutes later and saw that we were still in bed. He reached for the light switch and flicked it off without saying a word.

Good, I can sleep a little longer, I thought.

After a few minutes, Becky got up and turned the light on. "We better get up, Rachel. We have school." We were in fourth grade that year.

Father walked by again and turned off the light.

"Okay, I guess we can sleep a little longer," Becky said, yawning, and lay back down.

After another ten minutes, it was my turn to get up and switch the light on. But Father was back again in a flash to turn it off.

"Maybe there's no school today," I said and lay back down.

Becky and I had both fallen back asleep when Mother Barbara walked into our room. "Girls! School has already started! You're late!"

I rubbed the sleep from my eyes. "Father kept turning off the light, so we figured he wanted us to sleep."

"You can at least get up and help me with the dishes," Mother Barbara said.

We got dressed and went to the kitchen, working quickly to wipe down the counters and load the dishwasher. The day looked temptingly sunny and warm, and we wanted to get outside as soon as we could.

The phone rang. Mother answered, said "Yes" and "No" a few times, and hung up.

"Father wants you two to go to school."

"But we're too late now. Why did he keep turning our light off?"

"I don't know, but go get your books and get going."

I could tell Mother Barbara felt bad for us, but she was as afraid of disobeying Father as we were.

On the way to school, I had an idea. "Let's walk really slow, Becky, so we don't get there until it's time for recess. Then we can slip in and put our books in our desk, and it will be like we were there all along when everyone comes back inside." So we dawdled, stopping to look at the dogs in the kennels and the chickens in the coop. Five minutes before recess, we hurried to our classroom. Our teacher, Ora Steed Jeffs, was there helping a student with homework. Ora was one of Grandfather's wives, and she was very beautiful. Father was very fond of her, and often had her in his office for long private meetings. (After Grandfather died, about eight years later, Father married her as well as a number of Grandfather's other wives.)

"Why don't you girls go outside with the other children?" Mrs. Jeffs said.

Out on the lawn in back of the school, our classmates were playing Steal the Flag, and we joined right in, but in no time Mrs. Jeffs came out to get us. "Your father wants to see you."

We followed Mrs. Jeffs upstairs to Father's office.

"I want you to give these girls an F on their Attitude and Behavior reports today," Father said to her. To us he said, "You are the principal's daughters and should set a good example for other students, but today you set a very bad example by being late."

We both said, "Okay," and followed Mrs. Jeffs out. We were barely back in the classroom when Father summoned us back to his office.

"You girls are expelled from school. You were not only late and set a bad example, but you don't act like you even feel bad about it. Gather up your schoolbooks and go home. You can't come back to school until I say so."

Father isn't thinking straight, I thought. I didn't dare say so to Becky, but I had a feeling she thought the same thing.

That same night, there was a fire at Uncle Ron Rohbock's house, and Father was called away to help the family. I had a feeling the distraction and lack of sleep would work in our favor, and with that in mind, the next morning I said to Becky, "I bet Father forgot he expelled us—let's just go to school." Becky and I were seated at our desks by 7:15 sharp, and school proceeded as if nothing had ever happened.

The next time Father called me to his office during school, it was to admonish me for something completely different. "Your teacher tells me that two boys in your class are paying special attention to you. You must not encourage it. The worst thing that can happen is to let a boy touch you. Do you understand?"

"Yes, Father," I said.

Someone was lifting me from my bed. "What's happening!"

"Shh, shh. Rachel, you're okay," Father said as he stood me

up. I could barely see him in the darkness. He should have been doing night watch for Grandfather. The other girls were sleeping.

"Come with me," Father said, taking my arm and leading me out into the hall and upstairs to the living room. The house was silent.

"You act like you haven't been feeling well lately," Father said as he sat me on the couch and took my hands in his. "I thought I would rub on you a little bit." He lay me on the floor and lifted my nightgown.

Something inside my heart broke.

"You can go back to bed," Father said, when he was finished doing what he wanted to do with me. I fled to my mother's room, where I knew I was safe. I sat carefully on the edge of her bed, trying not to disturb her, but I began to cry and she woke up.

"What happened? Why are you crying?"

I didn't dare tell her. I couldn't imagine what Father would say or do to her, or to me.

"Rachel, you will tell me what happened."

I couldn't catch my breath from crying. All I could say at first was, "Father . . ."

"Did he hurt you? Tell me!"

I finally calmed down enough to tell her that he'd been touching me and making me do things to him. I didn't even know how to describe it.

My mother's lips pinched together; I could see she was furious.

"That is not okay," she said, got out of bed, and walked out of the room. I heard her walk downstairs to Father's bedroom. I lay on Mother's sofa, awake, all that night, listening to the sounds of the house. Mother didn't return until morning, and when she did, she went about her routine as usual. She never spoke of what I had said to her again, and I never found out what Father said to her, but whatever it was, it served to silence her.

I stayed close to Becky all that day, which we spent building cities and roads and mountains in the sandbox.

I was spared Father's attentions for about a week, before he summoned me again. The only difference was that from then on he would say, "You don't need to tell your mother, or anyone else, about this."

One day, when I was eleven years old and Father had me naked in his office while he touched me, he said, "Rachel, do you ever look at yourself in the mirror when you are undressed?"

I looked at him, his hands between my legs. After a few silent seconds, I said, "Yes, of course."

"I'm sure you get curious about how your body is changing and what it looks like, but it is wrong for a girl to look at her changing body in the mirror," Father said. "Your body is not for you. Your body is sacred, and it is changing so you can become a mother. You must never look at yourself in the mirror when you are undressed."

I ignored him and continued to look at my undressed body in the mirror. If nothing else, it was hard not to, since the bathtub was smack in front of the mirror.

Sometimes he took me to the school library instead of his office. He would undress me and then have me turn around so he could look at me and touch me all over, saying, "See, Rachel, I would never hurt you."

As I got older, Father would increasingly insist that I undress for him rather than make him do it, but I often refused, so he would undress me himself. Once, in his office, after he had me undress and then undressed himself in the closet, he had me lie on the ground with my butt up and my head on the floor. He lay on top of me, naked. I was terrified that he was going to "commit adultery" with me, but he was careful to not cross that line: he never went inside me with his penis, only with his fingers.

People around Father began to wonder why he seemed to favor my company far more than any of his other children. Mother Annette said to me, "Rachel, why don't you ask Father to take some of the other girls instead of you all the time?"

One evening in May 1995, Father asked Mother Brenda if she would tend the children while he took his other ladies to a late dinner being served at the school. My older sisters, Maryanne and Sandra, were going to help serve the meal, which meant I would be the oldest child at home. This was not the first time Father had taken his other ladies somewhere special and left Mother Brenda behind. She couldn't protest to Father, so she took it out on us children. That night, after Father and the other mothers left, I decided it would be wise to stay out of Mother Brenda's way.

As soon as we girls finished cleaning up after dinner, I pulled Becky aside. "Let's go play in the woods."

We snuck our pillows outside and climbed the tallest tree in the yard. We each perched on a high branch above the wall that encircled our property, using our pillows as seat cushions.

"I love it up here," I said. "You can see everything."

As my sisters Angela, Shirley, and Melanie were all trying to climb the tree behind us, I heard Brenda yell from inside, "You girls! You get out of that tree! Come inside for family prayer. It's time for bed."

"It seems way too early for bed," I said. "The sun is still up."

"Let's stay out here a little longer," Becky said.

We talked about the mountains and the neighbor boy playing

ball down the street, and enjoyed the feeling of the breeze in our hair.

"I'm going to tell Father that you are disobeying!" Mother Brenda was yelling now.

"I guess she's pretty mad," I said. "We better go in."

We climbed down with our pillows and went inside, ran to the living room, and got on our knees in a circle for prayer. The stern look on Mother Brenda's face struck us as kind of funny. We closed our eyes as we were supposed to, but we struggled not to giggle as she began saying the prayer. Suddenly our brother Mosiah ran in and jumped into the middle of the circle and ripped a big fart. That was no match for the smothered giggles of five silly girls. I pretended to cough to cover up my laughter. I heard Becky clear her throat with the same intent. I didn't dare peek at her for fear I'd burst into open laughter.

Mother Brenda finished the prayer without saying "Amen." She looked around the circle, furious. She grabbed Becky by the back of the neck. "All of you children, go to bed now!" She dragged Becky off to our room. She was always hardest on Becky, even though we were all equally guilty of disrespecting her. (I wouldn't understand until I was in a polygamous marriage myself that Brenda was probably jealous of Mother Annette as Father's first wife, so she took it out on Annette's daughter.)

The rest of us followed behind. I joined Becky, and Melanie and Shirley went next door to their room, while Angela went to lie on the bed in Mother Annette's room. Becky opened our window, picked up a book of hymns, stuck her head out, and began singing "When Upon Life's Billows." Shirley opened *their* window, stuck her head out, and began singing along with Becky. Then Melanie and I joined in.

Meanwhile, Mother Brenda went to check on Angela and found

her on the phone, trying to call Father to complain that we had been sent to bed too early. That's when Brenda heard us singing. When we got to the chorus, we started really belting it out:

Count your blessings, name them one by one
Count your blessings, see what God has done

Brenda came storming into our room, grabbed Becky by her hair, and pulled her in from the window. I jumped down onto my bed before she could grab me. Brenda stuck her head out our window and yelled over to Shirley, who was hanging out her bedroom window, "I'm going to spank you!" Then, turning her attention back to us, she shoved Becky over to her bed and smacked her across the face. "Father is going to hear about this," she snarled.

Becky was playing tough and wouldn't cry, but I did.

"I hate you!" I yelled.

Mother Brenda looked at me, shocked. I was not the kind of child who would say something like that, but at the moment I meant it for what she had done to Becky. I could tell Mother Brenda felt my words clear to her heart by the look on her face as she turned to walk out of our room.

Father called the whole family together the next morning.

"The Lord said, when you sin in public, you should be punished publicly. I got a report that last night you girls sinned in public by disobeying the mother I left to tend you, and then were disrespectful and rude. I want all the mothers and children to see how wrong you were."

Father picked up a yardstick.

"Becky, you will receive your punishment first because you were the most disobedient. Come here."

Becky stepped over to him, and he began whacking her legs. She wouldn't cry, so Father hit her harder. She still wouldn't cry.

"You're playing tough girl? Well, we'll see." Father continued hitting her harder and harder until, *SNAP!* The yardstick broke. But Becky didn't break.

Mother Annette started to cry and walked out of the room. I turned my head to look out the window so I wouldn't have to watch as Father spanked Melanie, Shirley, and Angela in age order. Then Father turned to me.

"I'm not going to spank you, because you are now too old for me to spank, but I want you to know that I'm very disappointed in you."

To the family, it probably looked like he was playing favorites, since Becky and I were the same age, but I knew in my heart it was because of what he did to me in secret. Father liked to reserve his punishment of me for when I disobeyed him till then.

4

Rebellion

By 1997 Father had six wives and the house was bursting at the seams with children, so he arranged for our house to undergo a major renovation and expansion. Church members donated a lot of time and money to make this possible.

When the construction was finished, there were fourteen bedrooms and the new kitchen was enormous, with all new oak cabinets, a commercial stove, a walk-in refrigerator, and white tile flooring. There were custom-made oak tables with benches in the huge new dining room so that the whole family could eat together. Even the living room got a total makeover, with beautiful green carpet and cream curtains, and new couches. There was a lovely new piano too. I was so excited that our house was so beautiful after all those years of mismatched secondhand stuff.

The work done on the outside made me sad, though. The workers had torn out the trees we used to climb, the fruit trees we used to eat from, and the beautiful rosebushes I'd so loved. Now there was just the solid cement wall circling the property, with some newly planted small trees and shrubs. The "woods," where we'd spent so much time as children, were no more.

Father seemed to be paying more and more attention to how we girls were maturing. One evening we were sitting in the living room as a family after the youngest children were in bed. Becky stood up and said, "I'm going to go shower." A few minutes later, she walked back through the living room on the way to the bathroom with her clothing and shower items in her arms. As she passed the couch, she dropped her deodorant.

"What is that?" Father said. "Bring it over here."

Becky picked it up and brought it to Father. He turned it over in his hand, his brow furrowed. "Have I approved this? I don't remember approving you to use such things. I want you to come talk to me about this after you shower." (Becky never did go talk to him that night.)

Father was against anything that made us smell good. Perfume was a sin, created so that women could tempt men to be immoral with them, according to him.

"Rachel, you can't comb your hair like that. It will make the boys look at you," Father said to me more than once the year I turned thirteen. I still braided it according to the rules of the church, but he didn't like how I did it in the front. He corrected me often about my appearance, but I was persistent in my disobedience. As our family grew, Father had less time to focus on me, and I was more and more determined to be a normal teenager, although I chose my battles carefully, since Father could still deny me access to the few pleasures I had, such as playing with my sisters.

But my hair was so crossing the line for Father that he actually expelled me from school for it, and I missed most of seventh grade. Father wanted me to continue my schoolwork at home, without a teacher, but I refused—instead, I spent a lot of time practicing my violin, playing basketball, or reading novels if I could sneak them. By then Father had forbidden gentile books entirely, saying that we could only read "priesthood books," which meant scripture. But every once in a while, one of us girls would get our hands on a gentile book at school or from one of our friends. That's when I learned the best place to read was the mud bathroom, the only place in the house it was okay to be behind a locked door. The only downside is that the toilet seat was really uncomfortable and cold, and sometimes I thought the ring around my butt would be permanent.

I increasingly felt I couldn't trust anyone, and I was always angry. I didn't even get along with Becky, who had always been my go-to person when I wanted to share a confidence or get comfort. More and more, I resisted Father's efforts to be alone with me, even as they became more brazen.

One morning before school, Father asked me to go outside to check the sprinklers with him. Standing in the yard, he grabbed my hand and put it in his pocket. I quickly realized there was a hole in the fabric as he pressed my hand around his penis, which was already hard. Father continued to hold my hand there as he walked around the yard, supposedly checking the sprinklers. A few of the younger children were playing in the yard. I knew they wouldn't notice or understand if they did; still, I was embarrassed and ashamed. We walked around like this for what seemed like an eternity. I tried to pull my hand away several times, but he gripped it firmly to keep me there.

"Well, it looks like these sprinklers are all working," Father said finally, and let go of my hand.

I tried to avoid him for the next few days, but I knew I couldn't avoid him forever.

In February 1997 I asked Father if I could get a dog. We had always had German shepherds around, and I still missed Sunny, but the ones we had now were mostly guard dogs for the family. I wanted my own pet.

"If you touch me right here," Father said, pointing to his crotch, "I'll get you a dog."

I turned my back to him. *Why is this the only way he will be kind to me? Will he ever stop doing this to me?* I knew I would have to give in. He did get me the dog, and I loved it, but whenever I thought about what I'd had to do to get it, I shuddered.

Mostly, I continued to disobey Father when I could, so Father punished me by leaving me at home when he took my sisters on vacation or out to restaurants. The family looked at me in wonder. *How does she dare disobey Father so much?* I knew I could never tell them the reason. Father had been very clear on this point: if I told anyone, I would lose all hope of having anything good in my life, common blessings like clothing and personal needs. If I wanted him to choose a good husband for me down the road, I knew I had to stay in his good graces.

Father wrote me a letter that year, explaining that I needed to get in the habit of praying to Heavenly Father if I wanted good things in life. If the prayers didn't work, then something in my life wasn't right. He told me he loved me and that he wanted me "to be a good clean girl that will be useful to the Prophet."

And still, Father's abuse of me continued.

"The Lord wants us to move to Short Creek before the year 2000 to protect us from the coming destructions," Father announced in September 1998.

For years we had been told the world would be destroyed in 2000, and only the righteous would survive. Father held this threat over our heads to make us obey him. I grew up believing I would die that year because there was no possible way I could be good enough to be saved. Even something as minor as arguing with my sisters or complaining about chores meant I was doomed.

But even the promise of salvation didn't mean I wanted to move to Short Creek. I hated the desert.

Father's announcement came just a few weeks after Grandfather Rulon had a stroke that left him incapacitated. Grandfather was still the Prophet, but Father started running the church from then on. Father would "consult" with Grandfather on decisions regarding the church and its members, but he wouldn't allow anyone else to speak to or see Grandfather. It was only through Father that we learned of the Prophet's revelations. Father had been ordained to the office of first counselor to the president of the Fundamentalist Church of Jesus Christ of Latter-Day Saints, which basically made him the Prophet's right-hand man. I knew that a person must be righteous to hold an office in the church. I wondered how God had let this happen.

Short Creek straddles the border between Arizona and Utah and is comprised of the twin cities of Colorado City, Arizona, and Hildale, Utah. It's completely isolated, with massive cliffs to the north and the Grand Canyon to the south, so just one main highway goes through town. The FLDS church leadership liked that; it made it much easier to monitor who was coming and going.

Short Creek had started as a small ranching community at the beginning of the twentieth century, but Mormon fundamentalists started settling there in the 1920s, hoping to practice polygamy in peace. It didn't work out like that. In the 1950s the governor of Arizona, John Howard Pyle, sent the National Guard into the community to stop the polygamy, which was a felony, according to state law. The guardsmen arrested the entire population of the town, including the children. Some children were kept away from their parents for as long as two years, and some were never returned at all. The governor made the mistake of inviting the press to witness the raid, and the sight of children playing in their yards being taken into custody did not make journalists sympathetic. Subsequently the governor was voted out of office, and after that the fundamentalist Mormon community was largely left alone.

By the time Father told us we were to move to Short Creek ourselves, most FLDS followers were already living there. Becky and I thought Short Creekers were "bummy and junky," and we swore not to be friends with them for fear we too would become weird. Becky complained that all that sand and red dirt meant we'd never have a neat day again too.

In those last few days in Utah we went on a lot of hikes, and took lots of pictures of our home and the mountains as keepsakes. It was autumn, and the leaves were making a showy display of red and orange and gold.

"I'll never forget how beautiful it is here," I said to Becky one day as we picked wild raspberries and sat in the tall grass.

"Or how much fun we had," Becky said.

It took all of September and October to pack up and get ready to move. By this time, Father's family numbered thirty-one members, with seven mothers and twenty-three children all living under one roof.

Most of the family left for Short Creek the last weekend in October. I wanted to stay in Salt Lake as long as possible, so I asked Father if I could go with the last ride. Father usually let me have what I wanted, like some kind of silent reinforcement for my keeping quiet.

On a rainy November 1, 1998, my sisters Becky and Maryanne,

Mother Barbara, and I were the last of the family to leave Salt Lake Valley. Snow capped the tops of the mountains, showing the first sign of winter. It was so hard to say good-bye.

"I don't think we can be as happy in Short Creek as we were here," I said as we started the drive south.

"I know we can't," Becky said.

"We'll make it fun," Maryanne said in her usual enthusiastic way. Becky and I looked at each other and rolled our eyes.

Three days later I turned fifteen, a milestone I marked by baking my own birthday cake. Father gave both Becky, whose birthday was two months later, and me beautiful cedar hope chests. Inside were baby clothes and dishes—a hint of our impending futures as wives and mothers.

Since Father's elevation to first counselor, our family now had some money, and Father spared no expense building us a huge new home in Short Creek. The house had seventeen bedrooms, but with so many children now, doubling up was a luxury we no longer had. Sandra now shared a room with Becky and me. The enormous kitchen had a huge commercial stove, an industrial dishwasher, and three large refrigerators. There were now three long custom-made oak tables to accommodate the family at mealtimes, and three long couches in the living room, but it was Father's big green recliner that took center stage. The piano was situated by his chair so he could guide whoever was playing in the songs he wanted to hear. Music was very important to him, and we had a family sing every Sunday night, although it was limited to hymns and devotional music we composed ourselves.

Outside, Father had the workers build a basketball court, and a sandbox with swings to keep the increasing numbers of children occupied. There was also a landscaped yard and a fenced-in garden where we would grow fruits and vegetables.

The property was connected to Grandfather Rulon's, with just a short path between our house and his. There was a trampoline in Grandfather's yard that we girls would jump on whenever we could; Father wouldn't allow us to have one of our own.

I had stopped going to school after eighth grade, but the year we moved to Short Creek I began teaching third grade at the church school, Jeffs Academy (I taught physical education to other classes as well). My little sister Teresa was in my class. She had the most beautiful strawberry-blond hair and tiny nose with freckles splashed across it. I adored her, but I loved all my other students as well, and I like to think that they loved me. All the teachers at the school were volunteers, so we received no pay. Father was still the principal, as he had been at Alta Academy, and still taught the morning class, but now he was also busy with church business, so math and the other classes he used to teach were now taught by someone else.

Father was also busier at home. He took ten new wives in 1999, which was a big adjustment for the whole family. Some of the new wives were as young as me, sixteen, yet Father's children were required to call all of his wives "mother." Some of these new wives became our friends, and others chose to inhabit the role of mother to the fullest extent they were able.

Jennifer and Joanna Steed married Father in October that year. Joanna was particularly naive, and Becky and I took every opportunity to tease her. We weren't mean, but we had our fun.

Two days after Joanna came to live with us, I went to her and said, "Father wants me to tend you today."

"Really? Does he not trust me?" Joanna said.

"I don't know. He just asked me to tend you today. We're supposed to watch over you, make sure you do good things, and don't get in trouble. Right, Becky?"

"He's anxious that we keep a good eye on you," Becky said.

"I don't plan on getting in trouble," Joanna said, a little disconcerted.

"Don't worry, it's not that. He just has so many wives to keep track of," I said, trying not to giggle.

Becky and I spent the day with Mother Joanna, taking her on walks, swinging on the swings, going to the grocery store.

Every night after dinner, Father conducted family class with Grandfather's family up at Grandfather's house. At a little before the 8:00 p.m. start time, we corralled Mother Joanna to go with us to class. "Father is going to be so proud of you when he gets our report," Becky said as we walked along the path.

The class lasted about ninety minutes. Afterward Mother Joanna approached Father and said, "Warren, what do I need to do so that you will trust me enough to not get tended?"

Before Father could say anything, I jumped in and said, "She did really well. I think she won't need a tender tomorrow." I gave Father a big smile.

Father quickly caught the joke and burst out laughing. "Joanna, did you really believe these girls were serious?"

Poor Joanna started crying and left the room, so Becky and I ran after her and apologized. "I never thought you'd believe me," I said, "but you went along with it so well, we didn't know what to do but keep pretending! I hope you forgive us."

Joanna started to laugh. "I guess that was stupid of me to believe you."

Joanna's sister, Jennifer, was one of the new wives who took the job of mother seriously, but it was hard for me to obey someone who was only two years older than me. One day when I was play-ing piano in the living room, she came in and ordered me to go help make lunch. I ignored her and kept playing. "I'm going to call Father and tell him you're not at your duties," Jennifer said. I gave her a look that said, "Get lost." Next thing I knew, I was being summoned to Father's office. When I got there, he asked why I was being disobedient to Mother Jennifer.

"She's basically my age. Why does she get to tell me what to do?"

Father sat quietly for a few minutes. This was new territory for him as well. "I understand, but I need you to respect my wives as a part of me. Can you do that for me?"

That evening at family class, Father addressed his wives. "I don't want any of my wives to treat my older daughters like chil-dren anymore. I want you to treat them as you would treat your sister wives."

I was grateful to Father for saying that. The wives became a lot more respectful of us girls from then on, especially when he started taking ladies who were even younger than us.

Father's attempts to be intimate with me grew less frequent as I got older and as he married more and more wives. It got to the point where I had almost convinced myself that he'd given it up.

He had not.

One evening Father took a few of us girls to St. George for dinner. Our car had bench seats, and he had me sit next to him in front while he drove, and my sisters were in the back. It was dark by the time we made the return trip home. I was just watching the road, not thinking about much at all, when Father took my hand and placed it on his groin. I tried to pull away, but he wouldn't let go. I was afraid my sisters might see, so I didn't dare fight too hard for my hand.

When we got home, I went straight to the bathroom and locked the door. I decided to take a long shower so Father wouldn't be able to get to me. Afterward I went to Becky and said, "Let's go sleep in Mother Barbara's room tonight." We'd often slept on the floor or sofa in her room while we were growing up. "I'll meet you there." I walked up to my mother's room and opened the door, only to witness Father and Mother having sex. Mother ran into her bathroom, and I ran back to my room.

"Becky, let's sleep in Mother Nette's room instead. Hurry, I'll be there."

A few minutes later, I was lying on Mother Annette's floor when Father came to the door. "Rachel, are you okay? Do you want to come talk to me?"

"No, I'm too tired," I said, and turned away from him to face the wall. I heard his footsteps as he walked away, and then heard him say, "Lori, come talk to me." Lori was one of his younger wives.

Several weeks later, Father announced to the family that both Mother Barbara and Mother Lori were pregnant and due on the same day. A wave of horror filled my heart. What if that had been me? I had a feeling that if I'd gone with Father that night, I could have been having a baby too.

Father tried one more time.

One night, in December 1999, Father called me on the house phone and said, "Rachel, come talk to me in my room." I had that warning feeling, but it was late, and I was too tired to disobey him.

I went to his room and knocked. Father opened the door,

motioned for me to step inside, and shut the door. The room was dark. Father took a seat on his sofa. "Come sit by me," he said. I sat down. He took my hand in his and caressed it gently. Then he put it on his "boy."

This time I didn't have to think about it. I was furious, and I was done with Father trying to hurt me. I quickly drew my hand back, got up, and walked out of the room, shutting the door behind me.

I went to my room, where a few of my sisters were being wild and silly, but I was in no mood to join in. Instead I picked up a notebook and searched our messy desk for a pen. I sat down to write Father a letter. I didn't know words like *molest* or *sexual abuse*, but I knew he would know full well what I was talking about. He would certainly understand when I wrote, "I hate you when you do those things to me."

I folded the paper and slid it under Father's door that night, then lay awake in fear of what he would do to me. The next morning, I stayed in bed. I did not go to morning reading and prayer with the family. I found out later Father hadn't gone that morning either, which was extremely rare for him.

Around 10:00 a.m. Mother Milly came to me. "Father wants you in his office," she said, meaning his office up at Grandfather Rulon's house, where he conducted church business.

My hands shook as I turned back the covers to get out of bed. Although I had eaten nothing since the night before, my stomach gurgled threateningly as though I would vomit. Usually I would make haste when Father had requested my presence in his office. That day my veins seemed filled with molasses, my movements awkward as I brushed my teeth and washed my face. I peered at my reflection in the bathroom mirror while I fixed my braid. None of Father's children had ever confronted him like this. No one in the entire church had done so. My future had never been so uncertain.

Walking up the path to Grandfather's house, I wondered what kind of father I would meet when I got there.

The door to Father's office was open when I arrived. Father was sitting in his chair. I stepped in, closed the door behind me, and took a seat right across from him, my hands in my lap. I did not want him to see the tremors that still plagued them.

Father looked at me in silence, a hurt showing in his eyes that I had never seen there before. I returned his gaze, undaunted. I was not going to offer comfort, if that was his expectation. We stayed like that for several minutes.

Finally Father's expression collapsed into one of shame and defeat. He dropped his gaze to the floor and took a deep breath. I could hear the catch in his throat.

Then slowly, Father slid from his chair and got down on his knees in front of me. He put his hands together, as though he was praying, and said in an almost ethereal, soft voice, "Rachel, please forgive me. I beg you to forgive me."

I swallowed hard to keep my emotions in check. I said nothing.

"Rachel, I beg for your forgiveness. Please, please forgive me."

Still, I held my tongue. The longer I did so, the more he begged. I began to feel embarrassed for him—not because he was prostrating himself before me but because this display of humility seemed hypocritical and insincere. I wanted to get up and run out of the room. Even his apology made me feel unclean.

"Yes, I forgive you." What else could I say? I had to stop this performance.

It worked. Father went back to his chair. When he looked at me again, his face had regained its composure. There was no hint of shame there anymore.

"Rachel, you are a good and clean girl," he said, "and I want you to know that my father put me in the position of first counselor, I did not. We can keep all this between you and me, okay?"

"Okay," I said. In truth, I didn't want anyone to know what had transpired in that office. It felt shaming.

Yet I felt a sense of relief when I left Father's office. I had a strong hope that the abuse was over, and I was free.

5

Keep Your Enemy Close

When the turn of the millennium came and went and the destructions that Father had promised didn't materialize, Father told us the world's calendar was off because God didn't want us to know the exact date of the destructions. It was the perfect way to keep the people sweet and on their toes in perpetuity.

I had lost track of the number of wives Father had; it had to be dozens by then. It seemed we were always getting a new mother. I was always kind to them, but I didn't go out of my way to get to know them individually.

In the meantime my two older sisters had gotten married, which left me the oldest of Father's children at home. I was feeling restless, so in August, just before the start of the school year, I asked Father if I could be his school assistant. He was still principal of the Jeffs Academy, but his duties as first counselor and de facto leader of the church took up much of his time.

We were sitting at the lunch table, and he looked across at me, his eyebrows raised in surprise. "Do you really want to?"

"Yes, really."

Ever since I had written that letter and Father had begged for my forgiveness—and my silence—I felt a sense of empowerment.

He could no longer hurt me, and if I asked for something, I knew he'd agree to it, if only to ensure the safety of his secret. I got as many favors out of Father as I could within reason.

"Come up to the office to talk to me about it after lunch," Father said.

Father put me through his assistant training, which I was glad to have. It helped me understand how Father thought and why he did what he did.

"Never make me repeat myself. Never say the word 'what' to me. Learn to listen very carefully to what I say. Never show your weakness to someone you have authority over, such as a teacher to a student or a parent to a child. Always make sure they respect you."

My job was to attend all of his school trainings, take notes, and transcribe his words. I ordered all of the school supplies, such as books and physical education equipment. I was Father's messenger to all of the teachers as well as the school recorder, keeping track of student enrollment and teacher staffing. When I had time, I substitute-taught classes as needed.

Father also gave me the keys to his bedroom and office, saying, "You will be the only other person with access to my private areas besides me."

"I don't want those," I said, but he insisted I keep them. When his sister Rachel had been his assistant, she'd had the same keys.

Over the next months Father kept me close to him, but he never tried to be intimate with me.

One of Father's duties for Grandfather was taking him on a long drive every day, up to four hours or even more, and Father would often have me join them on these rides. Sometimes Father asked me to drive *him*, alone, at night, so that he could get some sleep.

With more than thirty wives at home, this was the only way that Father could get any rest. I was not to tell anyone that I was driving him.

Father's wives grew increasingly jealous of the time I spent with him, which I didn't understand. I was no threat to them. I did not love Father as they did, and the memory of what he had done to me in the past still filled me with burning anger and hatred, although of course they knew nothing about that. I was just trying to spend my last years at home as a normal daughter, although the reason that he favored me so above his other daughters was never far from my mind.

6

Heavenly Father Offers a Blessing

"Becky, come sit by me for singing," I said to my sister as we were finishing our Sunday dinner, March 25, 2002. Every Sunday evening we spent an hour or two singing as a family.

"I'll be there in a minute," Becky said.

I ran upstairs and went to the bookshelf to get a songbook, and then took a seat next to my sister Angela on the couch. Becky came up and sat on the other couch, and we began to sing hymns like "More Holiness Give Me" and "Abide with Me." The younger children sang as loud (and flat) as they possibly could when we got to "Firm as the Mountains Around Us."

I enjoyed this time with my family. The warmth in that room made me forget the cool March night outdoors. I was as happy as I had ever been just then. I smiled at little Susie, two years old, going through her songbook, pretending that she could read the words.

"Rachel and Becky, I want your wedding dresses to be made by the end of this week," Father suddenly said. "Melanie's too."

I looked up from my hymn book. "Really, Father?"

He had a mischievous smile tugging at the corners of his mouth, so I wasn't sure if he was serious or just teasing us.

"When the Lord impresses me to do something, I do it," Father said.

"We don't want to get married," Becky said.

"Melanie can wait," he said. "Rachel and Becky, you can talk to me after prayer if you want."

Father had us sing a few more songs, but I could hardly focus on what we were singing. Father would choose our husbands, who might be our age or fifty years older, who might have no wives or ten or more wives, who probably would be people we didn't know. And we had no say in the matter. That made the prospect of getting married very scary.

Just before we knelt for family prayer Father said, "Rachel and Becky, I want you to know that if I could marry you I would. That is how special you are to me. If you weren't my daughters, you would be my wives."

I'm very grateful that I am your daughter.

Then Father said to the family, "Everyone treat these last few days with these girls very special." Becky started crying.

Father called on me to say the prayer.

"Heavenly Father . . . um . . ." I was so discombobulated, I didn't know what I was saying, but somehow I got through it.

After prayer, all the family went through the good-night line. There were so many of us that all of our daily rituals—meals, chores, and even saying good night—had become almost military in their precision. First we lined up in front of Father and one by one kissed his cheek. Then we shook hands with or hugged the other family members as we said good night to one another.

Becky was crying as we followed Father downstairs. He still had that grin on his face. He unlocked his bedroom door and invited us inside, then shut and locked the door. He sat on a chair and motioned for us to sit at the foot of his bed.

"You don't want to get married?" Father said to Becky.

"We want to wait till we get a little older," she said. Becky and I were eighteen. Some of father's newer wives were two or three years younger than us, so I didn't think this argument would persuade him. I did not like that he was marrying girls so young. It made me uncomfortable when I saw them streaming in and out of his room; I knew too well what he was doing with them.

"I'd love to keep you forever," Father said. "I love you both so much." He looked at me and said, "What do you want to do?"

I didn't really know, but I said, "I'm happy here, but if Heavenly Father is offering a blessing, I don't want to reject it."

"I guess I could keep you until you're twenty."

Becky stopped crying, assured that there were two more unmarried years ahead of us.

As we were leaving his room, Father said, "I still want your dresses done by the end of the week."

The next day Father sent Becky and me with Mother Barbara and Mother Annette into St. George, about an hour's drive to the west, to get some fabric. It was a hot day, even though it was only March. Leaves were sprouting on the trees and flowers were in bloom, but the red cliffs looked as dry as ever.

The mothers took us from one fabric store to another as we searched for the right fabric for our dresses. I wanted my dress to be as beautiful as I dared, with the best fabric, the best lace, and beads sewn onto the waist and yoke. After many hours and a lot of money, we went home satisfied.

I went straight up to Father's office and asked him if he would ask Mother Ora—the same Ora who had been our fourth-grade teacher (and also one of Grandfather's wives)—to sew my dress. She was an extremely talented seamstress, and I wanted my dress to be perfect. Father picked up the phone and called her. He said, "Take your fabric down to her room. She said she would start on it right away."

Mother Ora and I went over styles and patterns for an hour, as I explained how I wanted my dress to look. When I told her about the beads, she said, "We want to make it acceptable to your father."

"I don't think he'll mind," I said.

That night Becky, Angela, and I were sitting on the trampoline at Grandfather's, talking about our "scares."

"I'm sure glad Father isn't having us get married yet," Becky said.

"Why would Father be so eager for us to get our dresses done if we aren't getting married?" I said.

"What if you have to marry too old of a guy?" Angela said.

"We might have to say no to him, if he is too fat and ugly," I said. "Mother Ora has already started on my dress." I stood up and started jumping, bouncing the other girls up and down.

"I'm glad she's only working on yours," Becky said. "She doesn't have to worry about mine for a while!"

"Don't be so sure." I jumped harder. "Besides, I'm not getting married if you aren't."

"Quit it!" Angela said, trying to grab the skirt of my dress to hold me still. That just made me jump harder.

"He said he'd keep us till we're twenty," Becky said.

Angela got to her feet and tried to catch me, but I ducked out of her reach. Becky got up and tried to catch me, too, and we all started laughing and chasing each other around the trampoline, forgetting all about marriage for a moment.

Mother Ora was used to working fast; when Father decided there was going to be a wedding, there was no waiting. By Wednesday, she'd already completed the bodice for me to try on.

On Thursday morning, I was walking down the hall just as Father was leaving his room.

"Rachel, I'm presenting your and Becky's names to Grandfather at one o'clock today, so be prepared for anything."

I felt my heart leap into my throat. I knew Father would choose our husbands, since Grandfather wasn't well, but if Father was making a show of going to the Prophet, we were definitely getting married. I watched as he headed out the door. As soon as he was gone, I looked around to make sure Becky hadn't overheard what he'd said. If she knew he was serious about our getting married, she'd call him in Grandfather's office. I didn't want her trying to change his mind because I didn't want to be the only one getting married. I wanted Becky to share the fearsome journey with me.

I couldn't focus on anything the rest of the morning.

At 1:00 p.m., I found Becky having lunch in the dining room. "Hey, come outside with me for a minute," I said. She picked up her bowl of noodles and followed me out to the front porch, a place we'd dubbed "our spot," because it was our special place to talk about big "life" stuff. Most of the family never sat out there, so it was usually a safe bet we'd have it to ourselves.

We sat down next to each other on the top step.

"Father is presenting our names to Grandfather today," I said as calmly as I could.

Becky jumped up, dropping her bowl of food on the steps, and ran inside the house. "I have to call Father and tell him I don't want to get married!" she said as the door slammed shut behind her.

She came back a short time later. "Father's not answering the phone."

"Just because he's presenting our names, it doesn't automatically mean we are getting married. It just *might* mean that," I said.

"I hope you're right. We are not a bit ready for marriage."

"Let's talk about something else," I said. "I think it's awesome Mother Sharon is finally going to have a baby—"

"Me too, but I don't think you can distract me," Becky said. "I'm way too worried about getting married."

Just then Mother Vicki opened the door. She had a wide grin on her face. "Father is coming down the path, and he wants to see you girls."

Becky and I stood up and went inside. When I saw Father's big smile as he walked toward the front door, I knew that Becky and I were getting married; there was no question about it.

"Rachel and Becky, come to my room," Father said.

Twenty mothers, and thirty or more children, followed us to Father's room. Becky and I went inside while the family waited outside the door. Father sat in his chair, and we sat on two other small chairs on the other side of the bed.

He paused for a moment and then said, "Father wants you girls to get married tomorrow. I'm not going to tell you who it is. You will come to the wedding and be surprised, and your husbands will be surprised too."

I didn't say anything, and neither did Becky, but I didn't like not knowing who the men were that Father had chosen.

"Now let's go eat some lunch."

We followed Father to the lunch table. I wasn't hungry, and Becky was crying. Everyone else was smiling and laughing and talking about our "surprise husbands." We sat on a bench watching him eat, while he kept looking over at me, smiling.

"Rachel, you look so much like your husband," Father said.

"Does he have blond hair?"

"It's light."

"I want to know who it is," I said, emphasizing the word *want*. I had always imagined marrying a man with dark hair, but that wasn't the reason for the turmoil in my stomach. Father laughed and kept eating. When he was finished with his meal, Becky and I followed him back to his room.

"Did you girls want to talk to me?" he said as he unlocked the door.

"Father, we really want to know who we are marrying, just to prepare our hearts," I said. "If I'm to marry a short, fat guy, I'd like to be ready for that."

Father smiled silently for a moment. "Rachel is marrying young Richard Allred, and Becky is marrying David Allred."

Both of our husbands-to-be worked as guards for Grandfather Rulon. I had been a passenger in Rich's truck a few times when the family went on rides, but I had never given him a second thought. Father had said to us several months earlier that we would never marry an Allred because we were related to them through the Jeffs line. But I was also so very relieved—I was marrying a young man. I decided that I would be happy about this.

I hadn't even noticed that Becky was crying until I heard her say, "I can't get married to David Allred!"

Father was still talking. "Your husbands don't know that they are getting married, and we are not going to tell them. They will come to the wedding as guards and then be surprised."

I didn't really care if they knew or not, I was just glad that I did.

"Actually, do you want to meet them right now?" Father seemed to be enjoying our reactions.

"No, Father, please no!" Becky said. I was in agreement with her on this—it was too much to take in at once.

"I'll see if they are up at Grandfather's house. I want you to meet them."

Father called the house and made arrangements for the two men to meet him right away at his office. I couldn't believe how fast this was happening.

We walked with Father up the path. Becky was still crying. "Father, you said we could wait until we're twenty!"

"Are you worried, Rachel?" Father said to me over his shoulder.

"Yes, of course."

He laughed. He seemed to be finding this all very amusing.

When we got to Grandfather's house, Father took Becky into his office first, since David was already there and Richard was still on his way. I stood out in the hall by myself to wait. Then I saw Richard come through the door from the dining room into the living room. My heart started pounding so hard I could feel its beat in every inch of my body. I began sweating like I'd been running sprints. *I can't do this. This is way too scary. You don't just meet a guy and marry him!*

Rich didn't see me. He was combing his hair. I started feeling sick to my stomach.

Father's door opened, and Becky came out, her face white as a sheet. "That was terrible!" she whispered to me.

"Come in, Rachel," Father said.

I took a seat, and Father closed the door. I had been nervous in this room many times before, but this was completely different. I didn't feel dread, just a heightened sense of anticipation. I was about to meet the man I would spend the rest of my life with, and I didn't even know if I would like him. I was also scared of what Rich would think of me. Father walked over to the door on the other side of his office that led to the living room and opened it.

"Richard, come in here." As Rich got to the doorway, Father said, "Meet your new wife, Rachel."

Rich's mouth fell open as I stood up and clumsily shook his hand. I quickly retreated to the other side of the room and sat down.

Father said, "Get to know each other," and walked out, shutting the door behind him.

I sat in my chair, my legs swinging back and forth. I wasn't going to say a word unless he spoke first.

"Do you feel okay about this?" Rich asked.

"Yes." What else was I to say?

"How old are you?"

I realized I was acting like a little girl, so he probably thought I was very young.

"Eighteen."

We sat there for five minutes, neither one of us speaking. Finally Father rescued us by coming back in. "Rachel, sit right here," Father said, pointing to a chair next to Rich. I obediently got up and sat next to Rich. I started feeling very warm, almost dizzy.

Father sat in front of us on his chair and talked to us about being married. I was much too close to Rich to hear or remember much of anything that Father said, but I did catch him saying, "I want you to take Rachel alone to the wedding. Three hours together will be a good opportunity to get to know each other."

That scared me purple. Girls were forbidden to mingle with boys. The only man I had ever been alone with was Father.

I couldn't wait for this interview to be over, and soon it was. Rich had to go get ready for Grandfather's daily ride; he drove the bathroom trailer so that Grandfather always had a place to go, no matter how far afield they went. Father gave me some money to go to town and get wedding shoes.

Becky and I walked back home and told Mother Barbara that Father wanted us to get shoes. Mother went to get Mother Annette while Becky and I waited for them in the van. Angela came out to join us. "Mother said I can come too." Angela was our little tagalong, so we didn't mind.

The mothers came out and we drove off, but first they stopped at Grandfather's house. The mothers and Becky went inside. "I'll stay in the van with Angela," I said. I didn't want to run into Rich again.

"Who are you marrying, Rachel?" Angela asked. "Is he very neat?"

"I don't know if I want to tell you just yet. But he might be neat." I wanted to sort out how I felt about the whole situation by myself. Just then Rich drove up in his truck and parked next to the van. Talk about bum luck. I shrieked and threw myself down on the van floor to hide.

Angela started to laugh. "Now I know who it is!"

"Tell me when he drives away." There was no use pretending she wasn't right.

The ride to St. George was long, and all the talk of marriage wore me out. I barely had the energy or will to shop for shoes. Fortunately, I found a pair at the first store we went to, and Becky decided to borrow a pair when she couldn't find anything she liked.

When we got home, I got a phone call from Mother Ora. "Your dress is done. You can come and get it."

I went to her room and tried it on. She showed me how she had sewed each bead on by hand.

"Thank you so much for this," I said. "I like it very much. Will you be able to get Becky's done in time?"

"I hope so. Others are helping me with hers."

Back home, Father asked to see the dress on me. I wasn't really comfortable putting on an exhibition, but I relented, and I had some pictures taken with Mother and Father. Later, Father had Mother Ora remove some of the beads from the dress.

That night, as everyone was going to bed, Father said to me, "We'll be leaving around seven in the morning to go to the wedding. I want to talk to you before we leave, so be ready early."

My nerves were so agitated, I didn't know if I'd be able to get any rest that night. I put my nightgown on and got in bed, but I soon realized sleep was far from me. I got up and went to Mother Amy's room. She was one of Father's younger wives, just two years older than me, and we'd become close. "Please put me to sleep!" I said. She always knew how to make me relax.

"Of course I will. This is my last chance to do it," she said.

I lay on her bed and she rubbed my arms and legs in that way she had. Sleep finally came and relieved me of my anxiousness for a few hours.

7

Wedding

"I want you to get close to your husband quick. Ask him for a baby tonight," Father said in his office the morning of the wedding. How could I ask a man that I don't know a question like that?

Father was waiting for an answer. "Will you do it?"

I hesitated. I didn't like making promises I knew I wouldn't keep. "Uh, I'll try."

"No, not try. Do it."

I looked down at the floor, then back at Father. "Do I really have to?"

"Yes, I want you to ask tonight so you can get close quickly."

I very reluctantly said, "Okay, I will," and left the office.

I'd already spent more than an hour getting ready, putting on the traveling dress Mother Brenda had stayed up all night sewing for me. Mother Jennifer did my hair (way too tight). I was still worried about what Rich would think of me. I knew he had two other ladies already. I decided I couldn't be much shoddier than them. But now Father had made this daunting demand.

When Father and I left his office, Becky and David were in the hallway. I could hear a lot of commotion in the dining room. Father waved Rich over. "The grandmothers asked if you could walk in there together so they can enjoy seeing you." Becky and her man went in first, and then Rich took my hand in his. My heart did an extra ten beats. His hand was so large. I felt awkward standing so close to him. We walked into the dining room, and the grandmothers *ooh*ed and *aah*ed.

Rich walked me back out of the room and let go of my hand. "I need to get the trailer ready," he said.

I stood in the hallway, not knowing what to do next. My oldest sister, Maryanne, came over to me. "Rich's truck is down by Uncle Seth's house, so you'd better go."

"I don't dare!"

Maryanne laughed. "Come on, I'll walk you down there."

My next oldest sister, Sandra, was standing by our uncle Nephi's ride. "Sandra, what should I do? What do I say to him?" I asked.

"Just go get in the truck. It will work out."

I walked down to Rich's truck and climbed in on the passenger side. I was relieved that he wasn't there. I looked out the passenger-side window and waited. When I heard Rich get in on the driver's side, I looked over very quickly, then returned my gaze out my window.

Rich started the engine, and we set out. As we rounded the corner by the school, Rich's sister Jenny saw us and started jumping up and down. No one outside of Father's family was supposed to know we were getting married, but Jenny seemed very excited to learn our secret.

Rich stopped the truck back at Grandfather's house, and Father approached. Rich rolled down his window.

"Rachel, what are you sitting clear over there for? On the way back, you sit by your husband," Father said, pointing to the center of the bench seat.

I was about to spend three hours alone with a stranger I was about to marry. I couldn't think of a thing to say. Rich was silent too, which was a little surprising since he'd been through this twice before.

We were headed for the Caliente Hot Springs Motel in Caliente, Nevada, about 150 miles north of Las Vegas. The motel had been purchased by members of the church in 1997, and it was where all of our weddings were conducted until 2004. It wasn't fancy, but it was private, which was useful, especially when underage girls were getting married.

We must have been an hour into the drive when Rich finally spoke.

"Rachel, do you play piano?" he said.

"I do, but I'm better at the violin."

Those were the only words we exchanged for the whole ride.

When we arrived at the motel, I found Becky a sobbing mess. I felt like weeping too, but I decided that Becky was crying enough for both of us.

"That was the most terrible ride," Becky said. I felt the same.

There were six or seven weddings that day, and ours were to be the last two. Father was himself taking two new wives. Mary-anne, Sandra, Becky, and I were told to go to our designated room to get dressed and wait until it was our turn to get married.

While I put my dress on, I said, "Sandra, you have to help me. What do I say on the ride home? Help me think of something."

Sandra was lying on the bed, scratching her chin in thought. "Ask him about his accident."

"What accident?"

"When he wrecked his Jeep."

"Oh, right." I'd heard something about it when it happened three or four years earlier. Rich had broken his neck and had spent a long time in the hospital. It wasn't exactly happy newlywed con-versation, but it would have to do.

None of us could think of anything for Becky to ask her husband on the ride home, but we all tried to get her to stop crying before the ceremony. Even while she put her beautiful wedding dress on, while she undid her hair and rebraided it, the tears continued to flow.

Around two o'clock, Uncle Isaac knocked on the door. "We are ready for you girls."

We followed Isaac to Room 15, where the weddings were always conducted. Father and Grandfather Rulon were there already. It had been more than three years since Grandfather's stroke, and it showed. He didn't speak during the proceedings, just sat there quietly looking on.

There was an empty chair next to Rich, and an empty chair next to David. Becky and I took our places next to our future husbands. Father called Rich and me up first.

First he showed us the marriage grip, formally called the Patriarchal Grip, or the Sure Sign of the Nail. We clasped our right hands, locking our pinkies together and putting our index fingers on each other's wrists. I could feel Rich's large hand trembling.

I tried to listen carefully as Father said the words of the marriage covenant to Rich.

"Brother Richard, do you take Sister Rachel by the right hand and receive her unto yourself to be your lawful and wedded wife for time and all eternity, with a covenant and promise that you will observe and keep all the laws, rites, and ordinances pertaining to this Holy Order of Matrimony in the New and Everlasting Covenant? And this you do in the presence of God, angels, and these witness of our own free will and choice."

"I do," Rich said.

Father then said the same words to me.

"I do," I said, quietly.

"By virtue of the Holy Priesthood and the authority vested in me, I pronounce you, Richard, and you, Rachel, husband and wife for time and all eternity, and I seal upon you the blessings of the holy resurrection with power to come forth in the morning of the first resurrection clothed in glory, immortality, and eternal lives, and I seal upon you the blessings of kingdoms, thrones, principalities, powers, dominions, and exaltations, with all the blessings of Abraham, Isaac, and Jacob, and say unto you: Be fruitful and multiply and replenish the earth that you may have joy and rejoicing in the day of our Lord Jesus Christ."

Then Father said to Rich, "You may kiss the bride."

It was a very quick and awkward kiss. I could feel my whole face blush, and every nerve in my body tingled. Then it was over, and I was married. We returned to our chairs to witness Becky and David's nuptials.

As soon as the proceedings were complete, Becky and I went back to our room to change out of our wedding dresses, and then all the newlyweds and their families gathered outside for refreshments. It was nice to feel the fresh air against my skin after all the tension I had felt over the last twenty-four hours. We sat with Father and our family at a long picnic table, enjoying the day. Father was so excited about giving away his two daughters, he seemed to have completely forgotten his own new ladies. Rich and David, Becky's man, did not join us; they were getting things packed up for the return trip. I had a feeling they were glad to be out of the way for the time being.

When Father announced, "It's time to head back," my heart dropped into my tummy. I dreaded another long, silent ride with Rich. I could see plainly that he was as nervous as I was, which only made it worse for me. (Looking back now, I imagine his nerves were thanks to my being kin to the Prophet. That made marrying me a big responsibility for him, but that thought didn't cross my mind at the time.)

I got in the truck before Rich did, and took my place near the passenger door as I had on the way there. Rich climbed into the truck a minute or so later. I thought I was safe until Father came by and put his head in the window. "Rachel, scoot over."

I smiled weakly and shifted myself across the bench seat to the center, but I made sure that I was not touching Rich. Father smiled. "That's better."

I had never in my life sat that close to a man other than Father. I thought Rich could probably see my heart pounding through my clothing.

Ours was the third vehicle in the caravan of six. We drove several miles out of Caliente before I summoned the nerve to speak. "Will you tell me about when you broke your neck?" I was relieved my question came out as well as it did and I hadn't stumbled over my words.

Rich looked over at me, startled. "I don't like to talk about that very much." He paused for a moment. "But I think you should hear it." He drove on silently for a bit longer, as though he was working out how to begin. "It was May 1998, and—"

Flashing red-and-blue lights appeared in the rearview mirror. "Uh-oh."

Rich pulled off the road, and Uncle Isaac's voice came over the radio: "Tell him that you are just married, and he'll let you go."

Rich rolled down his window as the cop walked up. "You were going a little fast on this stretch of road. You were doing sixty-five in a fifty-five-mile-per-hour zone."

"I'm sorry, sir. I didn't notice the speed-limit change." I could imagine why Rich was distracted. My nerves were so jangled I'd have put the truck in a ditch if I'd been driving that day.

"Well, you be attentive," the cop said, and let us off with a warning. We hadn't had to mention the wedding.

Back on the road, Rich resumed his story. His Jeep had flipped over because he was driving too fast as he went over a cattle guard on a dirt road; the other guys were okay, but Rich had been knocked out. When he woke up, he realized immediately that something was wrong with his neck. He described the ambulance ride to the hospital, then being flown to a bigger trauma hospital in Salt Lake City. Grandfather Rulon had visited him there, and Rich had been very impressed by the man's greatness.

When Rich talked about his lowest time in the hospital, when he wondered if he would ever be himself again, he put his hand on my knee. His touch was gentle, but my skin seemed to burn under his fingers, and I started to tremble. Rich must have sensed my nerves, because he returned his hand to the steering wheel. I let out a breath and my muscles slowly relaxed. I didn't understand why his touch affected me so, and I suddenly found it hard to focus on his story; I had to force myself to pay attention.

"Does your neck still bother you some?"

"They had to fuse some of the vertebrae." Rich demonstrated that he could turn his head only so far. "And once in a while it reminds me I need to exercise it more, but for the most part I feel surprisingly well. The doctors said it would affect me more than it has."

The whole account made me feel tender toward him, but I didn't dare express it. As we continued on our journey, Rich shared some other experiences, and he talked about his testimony, how he believed that my grandfather Rulon was a true prophet of God. I believed that Rich's heart was good and sincere. My tongue also felt looser, and I asked him more questions that he freely answered. By the end of the drive, I didn't feel nervous anymore.

Maybe I would grow to love this man I was sitting so close to. My emotions were all weird and mixed up, and I couldn't place or understand them, but somewhere in the maelstrom I felt a spark of hope.

8

Love, Plural Style

As Rich and I arrived back in Short Creek shortly before sunset, I could feel my nerves start to dance again. The familiar road into town suddenly felt unfamiliar. Instead of making a left toward Father's house, where my family was, Rich turned right. I wondered who would be sleeping in my old bedroom now that Becky and I were both married. I wondered if Becky would be all right tonight.

"Our house is quite small for three ladies and three children," Rich said. He was smiling, but I heard trepidation in his voice. "It's not anything like what you are used to living in."

"That's fine," I said. I thought it couldn't be too bad—he did so much for Grandfather and Father, I was sure they would give him a nice house.

But as we drove up to his home, I was in for a surprise. Surely Rich Allred did not live in a place like this. The tiny house was run-down and shabby, the yard an unlandscaped mess, with horses and cows wandering around free.

I tried to hide my disappointment as best I could as Rich walked me up the steps to the front door and opened it. "Netta, here's your new mother," Rich said. "Her name is Mother Rachel." Two-year-old Jennetta ran over and hugged me around the legs. Rich then introduced me to his ladies, Trish and Molly, and showed me his two little babies, Rianna Joy and Sariah. They were both four months old.

Trish and Molly both hugged me and did their best to welcome me and act excited that I was there, but no wife is happy when her husband brings a new one home. And it was already cramped before I showed up.

Rich took me downstairs to show me around. "This is my room," he said. "The room upstairs is the ladies'. You can put your things in here for now, until we get more space." There was a single dresser, and he let me use one drawer.

I took in my new home: the wood in the walls was rotting; the bedrooms were tiny, even Rich's; the main living area consisted of a small kitchen with dark brown cabinets, cracked brown linoleum on the floor, and a small living room with faded blue carpet.

As the daughter of Warren Jeffs, not to mention the grand-daughter of Rulon Jeffs, the Prophet, I was probably spoiled. I had had everything I ever wanted. I had been so blessed until now that this seemed almost a humiliation to me.

I had brought only a small suitcase with a change of clothes and some personal care items. We would be going to Father's the next day to get the rest of my things. I stowed my few belongings and went back upstairs.

"Let's go over to Father's," Rich said. The family piled into his truck, and we drove over to the Allreds' house. Everyone seemed surprised and pleased to see us. I recognized a few people, but I didn't know anyone personally except some of the children whom I had taught in third grade. We were invited to stay for dinner, which Rich gladly accepted. We sat down to a meal of baked potatoes and salad, but I wasn't at all hungry. "Rachel, eat something," Rich said. I had just taken an oath to obey him, so I dished a small portion of salad onto my plate and forced myself to eat it while I listened to the family talk.

When we got back to our tiny house, I wondered how I would ever be able to call this place home. If I ran home to Father, he would only send me back. I knew I had to squelch my arrogance and accept my situation.

That evening Rich gathered his family for prayer. We knelt in unison, and Rich prayed. When we got off our knees, Rich said, "Rachel, come with me." We went downstairs.

I knew that the real time to be scared had arrived.

Rich shut the bedroom door behind me and invited me to get ready for bed. I went into the bathroom and put on my nightgown and robe. I sat on the bed while Rich used the bathroom. When he came out, he said, "Feel free to sleep however you want; you don't have to get under the blanket." My muscles unclenched. I'm sure Rich could see the relief on my face.

We each said our personal prayers, then he got under the blanket, and I lay awake and shivering on top.

Around 2:00 a.m., my new husband began to snore.

The next day Rich took me to Father's to gather my belongings. Becky was there with her man for the same reason, and my big sisters Maryanne and Sandra happened to be there too. While Becky and I were in our room packing, Maryanne and Sandra came in and shut the door. They looked at each other, half smiling and expectant.

"Do you girls know how you start out with a baby?" Maryanne said.

I was taken aback. Neither Maryanne nor Sandra were the kind of girls to ever talk of such things.

"Yes, we do," I said.

"Are you sure? Like, really truly?"

"Yes, really truly, we know," Becky said. Becky had asked me about it three years earlier, and I had told her because I didn't want Father to put her through what I had gone through when he was "teaching" me.

"Good, because if you didn't, we were going to tell you," Sandra said. "I was scared of my husband for a long time when he told me about it. I didn't want you to feel like that."

"Thank you for looking out for us," I said. "That is kind of you."

Later, Rich hauled my boxes and bins out to the truck. I wondered where he was going to put everything. He ended up loading most of it into the small rec room in the basement, and a few things in his room.

That night I decided I didn't want to freeze like I had the first night, so I got underneath the blanket. I thought hard about the question Father had instructed me to ask Rich. I hadn't found the courage the first night, but I wanted to keep my word to Father, because I still felt the need to obey him, although I feared Rich would think my question idiotic.

I took a deep breath, thinking about how to ask. The words wouldn't come. Then I simply said, "Father told me to ask you for a baby, but I wasn't brave enough to ask you last night."

I sensed him startle in the dark. "Do you even know how to start out with a baby?"

I told him what I told Maryanne, that I did.

Rich was quiet for a minute, then said, "Rachel, ask me when you truly want one."

While I didn't really want to go through the torture of asking again, I was grateful for the reprieve. No matter what Father wanted, I wasn't ready.

"Do you want to help me in the yard?" Rich asked at breakfast the next morning.

There didn't seem to be much of a yard, from what I had seen so far, but we went outside together anyway, with little Netta tagging along. There were a few large trees, their leaves still on the ground from the previous autumn. Rich went to the shed and brought out two rakes. "You can start in that corner," he said.

I was thinking over my new situation while I raked, annoyed that I couldn't organize my thoughts and feelings. I was weighing how I felt about my current circumstances: having no room of my own, stuck in a junky house, how different it felt to spend time with a man I didn't know, and trying to figure out my role as a sister wife. I paused at one point to watch Rich work. He got the hose out and started watering the trees, and I turned back to raking.

Then suddenly I felt water on my back. I quickly turned around to face him.

"What are you doing?" I said, backing away.

"I just thought you might want a little watering." He was wearing a mischievous smile.

I dropped my rake and ran across the yard, grabbing the hose into a big kink. Rich ran after me and tackled me to the ground.

"What makes you think you can do that?" I said.

"What makes you think I can't?" he said, his smile widening.

I tried to get up, but he held me fast. I reached with my one free hand and grabbed the hose to spray him a little, but he grabbed it back and sprayed me again. We tussled hard for about fifteen minutes. I didn't want him to think I was a weakling.

Both of us were pretty wet and cold by the time we stopped.

"Did I hurt you?" he asked as I sat on the wet grass, defeated.

"Not at all," I said with a smile.

He pulled me up onto my feet and gave me a hug. I squeezed him back and then looked up into his eyes. "Next time," I said with a chuckle, "it won't be so easy for you."

He laughed and said, "We'll see."

When we took Grandfather on his drive later that afternoon, I felt a warmth growing between Rich and me.

"How old are you?" I asked Rich on the drive.

"I just turned twenty-five in January. How old did you think I was?"

"Not twenty-five. I've never seen a man your age with three wives and three children already."

Rich smiled. "I'm just a little boy who does what he's told."

"How old did you think I was?" I asked.

"Younger than eighteen. Sixteen, maybe."

"Do I act young?"

"No, I just knew you were way too good for me. You and your sisters always had your noses in the air when anyone came around."

"We've always had each other for company, so we didn't try to befriend anyone else. We were actually the shy ones."

At this, Rich smiled and took my hand and placed it on his thigh, keeping his hand on top of mine for the rest of the ride. I liked how it felt.

No more jitters.

My sister wives didn't know that, although I was sharing our husband's bed some nights, nothing intimate was happening.

Rich never pressured me or attempted to touch me in a sexual way until I was ready.

Still, I could feel a lot of tension filling that little house. If I touched any of Rich's laundry, or anything else that belonged to him, the sister wives were quick to let me know that that was their job, and I wasn't supposed to touch his things. A lot of times they ignored me, or acted like I wasn't even in the room.

The worst times were the mornings after I had slept with Rich. His other wives were quick to say spiteful things to me, ignore me, or say rude things about me to Rich in my hearing. I was thrown by how unkind they were to me, especially since it was up to Rich to decide which wife shared his bed on any given night.

To make matters worse, on nights when I didn't share Rich's bed, I slept on the ratty secondhand couch in the living room, outside his bedroom. I really hated it, and it made me feel like I did not belong there. But there was nowhere else for me to go.

That Friday evening, while Rich and the family were sitting in the living room, I took the cordless phone outside to call my sister Sandra. As soon as she answered, I started crying.

"That's just how I felt after I'd been married a week," Sandra said. "You cry all you want."

I called Father next. Despite the fact that he had hurt me in the past, I still turned to him in times of need and trusted that he would help me as my father.

"How's it going?" he asked.

I had planned to be brave on this call, but I started crying again.

"Are you okay?" Father said. His kind tone made me cry harder, but I managed to choke out, "Yes, I think so."

"Tell me about your new home," he said.

I told him that I slept on the couch because there were only two bedrooms.

"For three ladies and three children? We better do something about that. I'll talk to Rich tomorrow."

"Thank you," I said between sobs.

"Rachel, be strong. It's okay to cry, but make sure you smile afterward. And remember, I love you."

The next night, Rich invited me to join him while he did night watch at Grandfather's. His job was to walk through the house and across the property, checking the gates and watching the security cameras to be sure there were no intruders. I couldn't say yes fast enough to his invitation. I was homesick and wanted to see my family.

"I need to talk to Mother," I said when we got there. "Can I run down to Father's house?"

"If you promise that you'll come back and that you'll still like me."

"I promise."

Rich looked so intently at me, it was like he was looking nearly through me. "Come here for a second."

I walked over to him, and he picked up a pen from the desk. He took my arm and pushed up my sleeve a little. He wrote on my skin, "I ♥ you." He looked up at me and smiled. I left the room feeling slightly . . . loved. But it didn't change my mind.

I ran down the path to Father's house. I was happy to be in familiar territory again.

"Are you hungry?" Mother Nicole, one of Father's young wives from Canada, said as I walked through the kitchen on my way to Mother's room.

"Yes!" I realized I was famished. "I haven't been able to eat much around Rich."

Mother Nicole laughed. "I'll warm up some spinach casserole for you."

I ran up to Mother's room. I felt such relief as I sat down on her couch.

"I'm glad to see you," my mother said. "What is that writing on your arm?"

I thought I had covered it with my sleeve. I felt my face get a little hot as I held out my arm so she could see, and she smiled. Soon Angela and Melanie joined us, and Mother Nicole brought up my food, which I ate eagerly between conversations. I felt so warm and comfortable, I didn't want to leave.

"Mother, may I use your phone?"

I called the living-room desk extension in Grandfather's house, where Rich was stationed.

"Can I sleep down here at Father's tonight?"

"Do you not want to go home?"

"I just feel like sleeping here."

Rich was quiet for a minute, then said, "Come up and talk to me," so I headed back to Grandfather's.

"Is there something I can do for you?" Rich said with concern in his voice.

"I don't know." I couldn't explain my mixed emotions, and I didn't want to cry in front of him. I really had no idea if he could help me or not.

Rich pulled me to him and kissed me lightly on the lips, and then let go. "You can sleep at your father's house tonight."

In the morning, Rich picked me up to drive me home. On the way he turned to me and said, "Don't let what the other ladies think or say bother you. If you know within yourself that you are doing what I want you to do, and that you love them, what they think or say shouldn't affect you. Heavenly Father's peace will be with you, as you live to do His will."

It wasn't until that moment that I understood that he recognized at least part of what I was struggling with.

"I want to be everyone's friend."

"I can see that in you, Rachel. But you have to remember, this is new for them too. Your uncle Nephi told me at our wedding, 'You're not really living plural marriage until you have three ladies. That is when the real tests come.' So give the other ladies room to grow and learn. They want to make this work, just like you and I do. We have to have open hearts, and we have to be full of love."

"Okay," I said in a whisper, tears threatening to return.

Then my husband put his arm around me and pulled me closer.

After family prayer that morning, Rich said, "Let's spend the morning together, all of us. We can have a picnic in the creek somewhere. Can you ladies get a lunch ready?"

I was grateful that he was making an effort to keep the peace.

Trish went to the store to purchase a few items while Molly and I got the girls ready. We drove down to the creek, and Rich chose a nice sandy area for a picnic while Trish and I made sandwiches. After we'd all eaten, Rich took off his shoes and socks and stood up.

"Come on, Rach, take off your shoes and socks. You've got to feel the sand between your toes."

"What if I don't want to?"

"Then I will help you," he said, and grabbed my foot. Rich took off my shoes and socks, picked me up, and carried me to the middle of the creek bed. I tried to wrestle away, but he was much stronger than me. We ran through the creek bed with Netta and Molly. Rich grabbed a handful of sand and put it down Molly's back, which started quite a sand fight. I backed off, not wanting sand down my pants.

When we were thoroughly sanded and sunburned, and the babies started wailing, we packed up and headed home. As Rich drove us home, I looked out the window and thought, We can have fun, all of us together. Maybe life as a plural wife wouldn't be so bad.

9

The Prophet Rises

It took me two months to summon up the nerve to ask Rich for a baby for real. I wasn't in love with him yet, but I did feel attracted to him. I thought if I had a baby with him, I'd feel love for him, although I didn't even know what that meant, to be in love with someone.

As Rich was leaving to do night watch at Grandfather's one evening, I said, "Can I come with you? I need to talk to you."

Rich hesitated for a moment, knowing that his other wives would be angry if he let me come. The picnic had not erased the animus my sister wives felt toward me or made them treat me any nicer. "Sneak out to my truck," Rich said. I knew sneaking was unnecessary; our house was so small, it wouldn't take long for the other ladies to notice I was missing. So I just walked out the front door, wondering why he couldn't be a man about what he wanted to do.

Father never cared what his wives thought of him. If he chose to favor one wife, he did so openly, in front of the whole family. It was no secret which of his wives were his favorites. Father was like a king in his household, and the women bowed to his every command. They stood around, eager for the privilege of handing him his spoon or washing the table after he'd finished eating. It was the highest honor to be the wife chosen to make his meal.

Rich didn't come out of the house for half an hour. I knew he was trying to make the other ladies feel okay about his taking me with him, giving them a little extra attention so they would feel special.

There was a big learning curve, living polygamy. As a sister wife, you might sleep with your husband one night out of six, or fourteen, or ninety, depending on your husband's whim. Rich was also on night watch a lot, so that reduced the opportunity as well.

The church teaches that it is good for a man to have multiple wives, so you cannot be angry at him for sleeping with his other wives. Living polygamy, you have to let go of your selfishness regarding your husband. You have to control the jealousy that comes naturally to us, not only because we are taught that jealousy is a grievous sin, but because it will make you crazy. But even though I grew up in this lifestyle, and I was used to it, once it became my reality as a sister wife, I realized how hard it was.

It took me an hour to finally tell Rich what I wanted that night.

"Really? Are you sure?" he said.

"I'm sure."

Rich was very pleased with my request, and happy to oblige.

He kept me with him for several nights in a row after that, trying for a baby. I found it very painful at first. Despite my past sexual experience, I had never done this part of it before. I was very scared and tense in the beginning, which probably made it even worse. I wanted to keep as many of my clothes on as possible, and Rich was kind and let me do as I pleased.

Life with my husband's other ladies got much harder then. Trish and Molly started to accuse Rich of favoritism, and would try to get in the way of our budding relationship. Nights when

Rich called me to his room, the other ladies would suddenly need to speak to him about "a very urgent matter." Sometimes they put little Netta to sleep in Rich's room so that nothing could happen between us. More than once, one of them would bang on the window so hard I thought the glass would break. At times I was angry that Rich allowed his other ladies to get between us.

And then, despite all their efforts, I was pregnant. I had been with my husband only three times; that's all it took. The church forbids husbands from having relations with a pregnant wife, so once my sister wives learned I was carrying a child, they stopped being jealous and mean to me, because they had him to themselves for the duration.

By then we had moved out of the tiny house that Rich had brought me to after our wedding. Father had taken my complaint about our cramped living situation seriously, for which I was very grateful. We were temporarily living in the basement apartment in Rich's father's house until a new house was built for us. The Allred house was fairly new, and the basement had four bedrooms and three bathrooms, so all of us ladies had our own rooms and we weren't in one another's business so much. But the jealous wives still kept close tabs on Rich, which was easy to do because the bathroom adjacent to Rich's room had two entrances, one from the bedroom and one from the hall, so whenever he was showering with one of his wives, anyone listening at the door could hear them talking.

I spent most of my time in my own room, since the apartment lacked a central living area. I liked having my own space, and it was comfortable. Father had bought a bedroom set for me because Rich couldn't afford one, so I had a queen-size bed, a nice oak dresser with a large mirror, and a nightstand. It was a lot better than the ratty old couch.

One night in late summer, when I was about four months along, Rich came by my room to say good night. We lay on the floor, talking. My feelings for him had grown a lot, and I had learned to trust him. So when he asked me that night how I knew about sex, I decided it was time to finally tell someone. I didn't dare share any details, not even how long it had gone on, because I feared what his reaction might be. I kept it short and vague; but it was enough.

Rich immediately stood up and left the room without saying anything. I wondered if I had made a terrible mistake. I lay on my bed and thought, *Rachel, you should have just kept quiet.* I tried to make myself go to sleep, but I couldn't because I was worried about what Rich was thinking about me after what I had told him.

A few hours later, Rich came back to my room and locked the door. He got undressed, and then he undressed me.

"If you weren't pregnant right now, I would be with you," he said. Rich held me close for a while, and I cried against his bare shoulder. It felt good to get even a tiny bit of my childhood hurt out. "But Rachel, please don't say any more," he said. "I don't want to know, because it will be too hard on my testimony of your father," meaning his belief that Father was a good and honorable priesthood man who stood next to the Prophet.

The next evening Rich called me from Grandfather's house, where he was on watch. "I wrote a letter to your father about what you told me. He wants to see us in his office right now."

My blood went cold. Father would be angry that I had told, and I didn't want to face him, but as always, I had no choice. I got in our family beater car and drove up to Grandfather's. When I got there, Rich took my hand, and we walked to Father's office.

"Richard, please close the door," Father said, and he gestured for us to take a seat. He gave me a look filled with hurt, as though to say, *How could you do this to me?* I looked down at my feet. Father still had full control over my life, and this betrayal surely meant he would never treat me the same again. He could do with me what he chose.

After a silence that seemed to last forever, Father said, "I always knew that I would one day have to talk to Rachel's husband about my relationship with her. And yes, I confess that in teaching Rachel, I got too close to her. I ask your forgiveness. Just know I am here to do my father's will."

Teaching? That's what that was?

Father shook both our hands and opened his office door.

"Thank you," Rich said to Father as we walked out. I said nothing.

When we got in the truck, Rich said, "Rachel, we have to trust that he is in a leading position for a reason. I don't ever want to question him again, so let's not talk about this." As it was my duty to obey my husband, I merely nodded my head. What small relief I'd felt confiding in Rich quickly faded.

A couple of things changed for Rich and me after that meeting with Father. The first affected Rich: Father made sure to make Rich feel needed and important to him, keeping him close by his side always, first as counselor and then by making him a bishop—a leader in the church. The second affected me: from then on, I was largely kept away from my own family. Months, sometimes years, would pass when I didn't have any contact with my closest sisters; Father required us to live states apart with no freedom to visit, write, or talk to one another.

Grandfather Rulon was admitted to the hospital on the evening of September 7, 2002, with an intestinal blockage that required surgery. By then he was eighty-six years old, and frail. Rich and I joined Father and a few other family members—Mother Mary, Uncle Nephi, Uncle Isaac, and one of Isaac's ladies—in the waiting room early the next morning, waiting for word from the surgeon. Father told us to pray and fast for Grandfather to be healed. Finally, the surgeon came out and reported that Grandfather was very weak after the surgery, and they weren't sure he was going to pull through.

"He is going to make it," Father said. "Make sure he makes it."

Around noon that day, the doctors reported that Grandfather was failing.

"You must do CPR," Father said. The medical team—doctors and nurses and technicians—worked for nearly an hour trying to save Grandfather. Father insisted they keep going. Father had promised the people many times that Grandfather would be renewed and become a young man again in this life. And when that happened, Father said, we, the people, had better be prepared for the "great lifting up," when the "destructions" would cover the land, and only the righteous would remain.

We were with Grandfather in the ICU when he died that afternoon.

Father cried. I had never seen Father cry before.

It was Sunday, so the people in Short Creek had gathered at the meeting house. Father called over there to announce Grandfather's passing. The members of the FLDS had been told that their leader would never die, that his renewal was necessary for their survival. Instead, now they would have to follow another.

Father had been acting leader of the church ever since Grandfather's stroke four years earlier, so the transition was perhaps less jarring than it might have been. Father had been making decisions and arranging marriages all that time with Grandfather's "counsel," and he was careful in announcing that he was their new leader, relying on the testimony of his brothers and Grandfather's wives to tell them.

But there was a catch: we had been taught that an apostle, like Grandfather, had to name the next apostle, and Grandfather had never ordained Father to the apostleship, and the people knew this. As always, Father had an explanation for everything. Not long after Grandfather's passing, Father told the people, God had come down into Father's bedroom and ordained him an apostle Himself. (That bedroom is considered sacred to this day.)

I hadn't forgotten what Father had said to me at Uncle Roy's funeral when I was a little girl: the Prophet is the greatest man on earth. The Prophet is the only man worthy of hearing God's word. I knew Father wasn't a good enough man.

Soon after that, Father went on the run.

Part Two

10

Plural Wife

After a half century during which the world mostly left our people alone, in 2003 the state of Utah started prosecuting FLDS members for bigamy and underage sex. As the leader of the church, and the person who performed most of the marriages, Father knew they'd be coming after him soon enough, so he started looking for new homes for our people, far from Short Creek.

Father often brought Rich and me with him on these travels. At first we stayed mostly in Utah, but we began going farther and farther away to remoter locations in other states. We'd stay at different hotels and motels; Rich or one of Father's other body-guards would get a room, and then Father would go in the back door to avoid being seen.

It was hard being on the road as my pregnancy progressed, but spending so much time with my husband, without the distraction of the other ladies, brought us even closer together.

The last time I went with Rich and Father on one of these scouting trips, we stayed at the Residence Inn in Durango, Colorado.

"How long until your due date?" Father asked me at breakfast in the hotel restaurant. He couldn't help but notice the size of my belly by then.

"Three weeks."

He sat back with a surprised look on his face. "We better get you back. You don't want to have your baby in a hospital."

I'd actually like *to have my baby in a hospital*, I thought, but Father's family were required to have their babies at home with an uncertified nurse/midwife whom we called Grandmother Sharon. She had delivered me nineteen years earlier.

"I'm okay," I told Father. "I haven't had any signs yet." Nevertheless, we made the six-hour drive back to Short Creek the next day.

When I went into labor a few weeks later, Rich took me up to Grandfather's house to deliver the baby. He told me he'd asked his other two ladies, Trish and Molly, to be there too, which made me really unhappy. My sister wives still didn't care for me, and I didn't know how they would feel about my baby.

The labor was difficult and long, and I had a large audience, which only made it worse. Aside from my sister wives and Rich, three of Father's ladies, plus my mother and grandmother, Merilyn, were all watching me. I felt like I was putting on a performance for them, and doing it badly. My baby was crowned for three hours, but I couldn't seem to push her out. *Surely they'll take me to the hospital soon*, I thought.

Unbeknownst to me at the time, Father was just outside the open door watching as well, and he told Rich to ask my sister wives to leave. I don't know how he had the awareness to do that, but it seemed to relieve some of the tension I was feeling. After they left, I was finally able to push the baby out, although not without tearing myself so badly that I needed forty stitches to put me back together.

I loved being a new mother. My baby daughter was everything to me. She was beautiful and cheerful and good-natured. As Father's third grandchild, she got a lot of love and attention from Father's family. But I was not allowed to name her. Father chose his grandchildren's names, and a week after she was born, he gave her a blessing and named her Barbara Ann Jeffs, after my mother.

Years earlier I had said to my mother, "I love you, but I don't love your name, so I will probably never name any of my children after you." I looked over at Mother during the blessing and tried to smile, but she knew I was disappointed. Immediately after the ceremony, I let it be known that I would call my daughter Barbie, because Barbara seemed too long a name for a tiny baby.

Two weeks after Barbie was born, Rich came to my room. The new house that Rich had built for our growing family was a major improvement over the crummy old one. This one had eight bedrooms, so we adults each had our own room with a private bath, and Rich let us choose the carpet for our rooms. Mine was rose pink.

"I have a strong feeling that we should be together now that you have had your baby," Rich said.

I was lying on my bed, resting, still sore from the delivery. The stitches had only recently come out, and I was just starting to heal, but I didn't dare tell him no, so I went with him to his room. Sex was agony, but he didn't seem to notice. "Rachel, I love you so much. I just wanted to show you," my husband said.

In April 2003 I went up to Father's house to find Rich. All the family members I encountered looked at me with sad expressions. What's the big deal? I wondered.

"Rachel, you need to go talk to Father," one of his wives said.

I walked down to Father's room and knocked on the door. "Come in," he said, and I sat down on the end of his bed. "What can I do for you?"

"I was told I need to come see you," I said.

Father sat there for a moment before he said, "It looks like your mother has breast cancer. A doctor has confirmed it."

I bolted from Father's room and ran up to Mother's room, where I found her lying in bed. Barbie was only two months old, and I had spent most of my time recently with her, so I hadn't seen how ill my mother had become. I was only nineteen, and my mother thirty-eight. (She had a two-year-old baby herself.)

Mother told me that she had noticed the lump in her breast two years before, but Father told her not to worry about it. After the cancer had grown considerably, Father finally let her get it looked at by a doctor. No one in the family went to the doctor without Father's permission. The doctor hadn't just confirmed her diagnosis; he'd told Mother that her condition was already terminal, and gave her six months to live.

Father told her to have the chemotherapy anyway.

In the weeks that followed, I accompanied Mother to her chemo appointments, but it seemed like all the medicine did was make her get sicker and lose her hair. Still, Father insisted she continue.

When Barbie was three months old, Rich was called on a special mission by Father. Rich was sworn to secrecy, so he wouldn't even tell his own family. He was gone for weeks, sometimes months, at a time, and when he came home, he'd be dressed like a gentile. Whatever Rich had been doing, it was clear that it had been important to blend in with the outside world.

Once Rich came home with a stylish beard and mustache, a knit shirt, and a cool hat. I loved it.

"You look awesome!"

"Oh, you think so, do you?" Rich said, and pulled me into his arms, tickling me. I laughed and tried to squirm away from him.

I was still negotiating the challenges of being a plural wife. When I was with Rich, I felt that we had that special husband-and-wife attachment, that he was truly my best friend. When he spent time with his other wives, I felt as though he had betrayed that friendship. I'm sure the other ladies felt the same. I'm sure they also wanted to take advantage of the time they got with their husband. Every time Rich and I were together, I wanted him to prove all over again that he loved me as much as he said he did. I'm sure all plural wives want to be the special one, the one the husband loves more than all the rest.

Life with my sister wives was especially challenging during this period. Rich was home for such a short time between trips away, and all the ladies wanted a piece of him. I had an outside door to my room, and sometimes Rich used it to sneak in and spend the night with me without the other ladies knowing. I felt a little bad for my sister wives, because I knew I wouldn't like to be left out, but I was also glad that Rich chose to make me feel special and wanted.

In August 2003 Rich sought me out in my room. "Go ask your father what you need to do so you can come on this special mission with me," he said. "He keeps telling me he is going to have you come with me." I still didn't know what his mission was.

"I don't dare," I said. "I know Father. He doesn't like people to ask him for a blessing."

"Rachel, just obey me and go ask him."

I tried to avoid it for a few days, but Rich kept telling me to ask Father, so finally I went up to Father's house and asked if I could speak with him.

"Rich wants me to ask what I need to do to be worthy to go with him."

Father scowled. "You never ask the priesthood for a blessing. You always wait for it to be offered."

It was exactly what I expected. I would suffer the consequences of my request soon enough.

In November of that same year, Father announced that the Lord had given him a new revelation. Father was to take all of his underage children to a special place in Texas that the Lord called a "land of refuge," which was designated only for the more worthy of his people.

I later learned that Father had found a property in Eldorado, Texas, a state where the age of consent for marriage was only fourteen at the time. Father had instructed David Allred, Rich's brother and my sister Becky's husband, to purchase the land for the church. There, Father had ordered construction of what would become the Yearning for Zion Ranch. Father himself would never live there, or anywhere, full-time, since he was always on the move, evading the law.

Mother Annette told us girls that Father gathered all the mothers of his children in his office to break the news. "The Lord has directed me to move my children to a sacred land. He has also shown me that none of you are worthy to go." The mothers would have to prove themselves before they could move. In their stead, Father selected several of his wives who were *not* the mothers to take care of the children. Why the childless wives were more worthy than the mothers was a mystery.

My mother, stricken by what this meant for her, given her cancer diagnosis, stood up and threw her arms around Father. "Warren, then I will never see my children again!"

Five of Mother's younger children would be sent away. My littlest sister, Amber, was just two, and my little brother Joseph was four.

Father, seemingly unmoved, said, "This is the Lord's will. This is what He wants me to do."

I was furious at Father, and sad for my mother. As a mother myself by then, I knew how angry and hurt I would have been if he had taken my children away.

Melanie and I, who were Mother's two oldest girls, and our brother Ammon, who was fifteen, were all she had left, and Melanie and I were both married and living in our husbands' homes. After Father sent the children away, I began taking Barbie, who was Mother's first grandchild, over to spend time with her every day. Mother loved Barbie and enjoyed reading books to her and singing to her, and I could see she found it a comfort to be with my little girl. Mother put all her love on Barbie to cope with the loss of her own children.

Still, Mother cried a lot, and her health declined quickly after her children were taken away. Some of the mothers were reunited with their children within a week, but others, including my mother, hardly ever saw their children again. She wasn't even allowed to talk to them on the phone.

Father never visited her either, and it wasn't because he was always on the road. He had been her husband for more than twenty years, and now it was as though he had put her out of his life.

That same month, November 2003, Rich came home with a surprise—he had a new wife. None of us ladies knew he was getting married again, not even my sister wife Molly, whose own sister Susan was the new bride.

I didn't know how to feel about the situation. I had been married to Rich for a year and eight months, and I had grown to love him. I went upstairs to my room, took my baby girl in my arms, and cried. I vowed that I would not treat this new wife the way the other ladies had treated me; I would treat her kindly, even if I didn't like her. But it was weird to think of Rich sleeping with a new girl, one that didn't even love him.

Father told Rich to take Susan with him on his mission to the land of refuge in Texas. I felt betrayed that Rich took someone else, especially after I had risked Father's anger by asking for a blessing so that I might go with him. As always, I did my best not to show it, since showing feelings like anger and jealousy was a sin. But I know my sister wife Trish felt the same way about not having been chosen. (My other sister wife, Molly, was just glad it was her sister who went and not me. In the coming years, Molly would often lobby Rich to favor her sister over me whenever she could.)

And then I discovered I was pregnant with my second child.

I focused on staying busy. I tried to work harder, be kinder, and love more to prove myself worthy of living with Rich. I saw my mother every day. Molly went to live with Rich in the land of refuge a month later, leaving just Trish and me and our children in Short Creek. I got along better with Trish without the others around. In fact, I felt that we were becoming friends, although I knew it was peaceful between us only because Rich wasn't there.

Mother continued to get sicker and sicker. In April 2004, Father allowed her two youngest children to come back to Short Creek to be with her, but she was too weak to do anything with them, let alone care for them. By May the cancer had spread to her lungs, and she was on oxygen to help her breathe.

"The Lord showed me that you have humbled yourself enough to be worthy to come to Zion," Father said at last. She would be moved to the Texas land of refuge to join the rest of her family, but she was in a wheelchair, and the treatment had knocked what life she had left right out of her.

"Mother, I really want you with me when I have my baby," I told her as we said our good-byes. Melanie, Ammon, and I were not allowed to go with her, as we were still unworthy.

Mother looked at my belly, which was just starting to get round, then back up at my face. "I probably won't be there," she said.

"Why? Why won't you?"

She smiled at me through her tears but said nothing.

Two months later, on July 8, Father called me. "Rachel, your mother is dying, and—" I didn't hear the words he said after that, only a voice in my head screaming "No!" Even knowing how sick she already was the last time I saw her, I couldn't accept it. *These kinds of things don't happen to us*, I thought. They happen to other people.

I tried to bring myself back to what Father was saying. "You are not worthy to go on the land where she lives, but you can come see her while she is in the hospital in San Angelo. Isaac will drive you." I wanted so much to talk to Rich, to cry on his shoulder, but that was impossible, as I had no way to reach him.

I packed a bag for Barbie and me, which was more difficult than it should have been because, at seven months along in my pregnancy, I felt big and tired. When Uncle Isaac picked me up, he told me I couldn't bring Barbie.

"But Mother will want to see her as much as me, maybe more. I have to bring her."

"Your father did not say she could come."

I was heartbroken for my mother. I was also leery of leaving my child with Trish, but I had no choice. It would be the first time I was separated from her since she was born.

Isaac had me sit in the back of the SUV with Ammon for the seventeen-hour drive to the hospital in San Angelo. It was one of the longest, most uncomfortable rides of my life. Three hours into the journey, Father called me on Isaac's cell phone.

"Is Barbie with you?"

I burst into tears. "No, Isaac said not to bring her."

"You left your little girl with your sister wife who hates you? Never do that. Call your sister Shirley and have her go get Barbie and take care of her until you return."

It took me a couple of minutes to get through, and when I did, Shirley had already spoken to Father and was on her way to get my daughter. I was still upset at Isaac for not letting me bring her like I wanted, but I felt grateful that Father cared about her welfare.

Mother looked like she had aged forty years in the few weeks since I'd last seen her. Lying in her hospital bed, she was terribly frail and had a faraway look in her eyes, like she was already partway gone to the other side. I didn't want her to see me cry, so I walked over to the window to hide my face until I got control of my emotions. When I calmed down, I went to her bedside.

"Hi, Mother. This is Rachel."

My mother continued to stare ahead. "Where's Barbie?" she whispered.

I started to cry again. I couldn't bring myself to tell her that I had been forbidden from bringing her namesake grandchild. I sat with her for an hour, and I could see she was failing fast. Uncle Nephi was there with us, and he made arrangements to have

Mother transported back home, as she had expressed her wish to die there.

Father called while we were still at the hospital. "This is the last time you and your brother will see your mother, because you are still not worthy to be on the land of refuge." We would not be allowed to go to her funeral.

Ammon and I were given a motel room that night, and a ride would come get us the next day. I couldn't sleep. I was devastated to think I wouldn't see my mother again. I don't think Ammon slept a wink either.

Every once in a while, I would say, "Ammon, are you still awake?"

"Yes," he'd say. Then after some more time passed, "Rachel, are you awake?"

We did that through the night, alone in our grief, knowing that our mother was near the end of her life and we couldn't be with her.

Father called in the morning with a new revelation. "The Lord showed me that seeing your mother dying has humbled you and Ammon enough that you can be trained and then go to your mother." It was a glimmer of hope, but it meant that Uncle Nephi had to drive us more than five hundred miles—an eight-hour journey—to Albuquerque, New Mexico, to meet Father. It wasn't lost on me that even as Mother was so close to death, Father didn't feel it was important for him to be with her.

It took Father all day to give us the "special training," in which he instructed us about strict obedience, hard work, no complaining, rising no later than 5:00 a.m., getting to priesthood trainings on time, no gentilism of any kind, wearing plain pastel clothing in the house and dark clothing when outside working, and no shoes inside. He told us the Lord wanted a temple built in Texas. Father had us covenant to do all the good things and to keep the land of refuge a secret and sacred place. Finally, we were deemed worthy.

When we arrived in Eldorado, after another daylong drive, I was surprised that Father had chosen such a barren desert to be a sacred land of refuge for our people. There was cactus and white rock everywhere. I didn't see anything beautiful about the place. Even the log cabins the men had built didn't match the landscape. The land was code named R17 (Refuge 17), since it was seventeen hours from Short Creek.

My little and big sisters ran out to meet us. I was so glad to see them, and they were happy that I had been proved worthy to come to their new home. They showed me up to Mother's room, but she was already in a coma.

"She kept asking after you and Ammon," my sister Maryanne said. "When we told her you were coming, she fell asleep and hasn't woken up since."

I took hold of Mother's hand. There was no stopping the tears now.

Father came to see her a few hours later. "Your mother is in God's hands," he said. One of Father's other wives had written a song a while back called "Father, Bless Dear Barbara," that Father wanted us to sing, but the song just made me cry, especially the line, "though we're tested until death." Father's wives had sung that song to my mother a few months earlier, and that line had caused her to weep and weep. I had felt then it was thoughtless of them to sing that to her, and I still thought so.

We sat with Mother all that night and into the morning, when the nurse had us step out so she could change Mother's bedclothes. That's when my mother's heart stopped beating.

Mother had just recently turned thirty-nine years old.

When I stepped back into the room, Mother was lying on the couch, where the nurse had laid her, with a slight smile on her face. She looked more like herself than she did when she was alive and racked with pain. I was filled with sadness, but also gratitude that she was relieved of her suffering, which in my heart I knew had been made worse because her children had been taken away from her for so long.

A little later, I asked Father if Rich was there. He told me that Rich was living on a different land of refuge in South Dakota, but that he was coming down to Texas for Mother's funeral. Father was also having Grandmother Merilyn and my half sister Sandra bring Barbie from Short Creek. Rich would take Barbie and me back with him to South Dakota together.

Several of father's wives got together to quickly sew white dresses for me and some of the other girls for the funeral the next day, while we practiced the songs that we would sing during the ceremony. Father encouraged everyone to wear white at funerals.

That afternoon, Rich arrived. I was so glad to see him after these months apart, and I think he was twice as happy to see me, especially since I'd be going back with him. Father's family gave us Mother's room to stay in, but I couldn't stand to be there. Everything in it was a reminder that she was gone.

Even with all the hustle and bustle getting things ready for the funeral, I noticed that my sister Josephine was missing and went looking for her. She was thirteen, Mother's fifth child. I thought about how I had struggled at that age, and how especially devastating losing our mother must be for her. I found her curled up asleep on the floor of a closet, her face red from crying, the tear tracks still damp on her face, and her thumb in her mouth. She hadn't sucked her thumb in years.

"Josie?" I knelt down and took her in my arms.

She opened her eyes a little, then quickly closed them as though she were trying to hold back her tears.

"I hope you know that I love you and am always here for you."

Josie kept weeping and sucking her thumb, obviously desperate for whatever comfort she could get. My heart broke for her and all of Mother's younger children, having to grow up without her. And the reality was, I would be living far away from them, too; I wouldn't be able to be there for them, no matter how much I wanted to be. Little Amber had just turned three; Joseph and Jacob were five and seven. How would they fend for themselves without a mother? Even with so many mothers, no one can replace one's own mother.

Father told me to go with Mother Annette and my sister Melanie to the mortuary to help dress Mother. I went with them, but when we got there, I couldn't bring myself to go in the room where her body was. I didn't want to remember her like that, so I stayed in the waiting area while they dressed her.

Sandra arrived with Barbie on the morning of July 10. Rich and I both couldn't stop hugging our little girl. Mother Milly had Barbie and me try on our dresses, and then we got our hair combed up for the funeral.

Father told us that only he would stand in the viewing line to receive people paying their respects. He did not want her children standing next to the casket or participating in the viewing line, because he didn't want the men shaking his girls' hands. He stood and shook the people's hands by himself, the mourning widower, even though he had not been with his late wife when she needed him most.

Father spoke for three long hours. No one else was invited to say anything, except for the few songs that we sang. He talked about how Mother was not a perfect wife, that she was jealous sometimes, and that the Lord gave her cancer to punish her. I didn't think I could cry more than I already had, but I felt so sorry for Mother then. I believe most of the people did, but saying so was not allowed. Father was hard on her, and he didn't want the people to feel bad for her. Rather, he said he was the one suffering, and that her illness had been difficult for him. He went on to say that in the end her cancer had humbled her and made her worthy of salvation, and that she had sacrificed her life so that her unworthy children (Ammon and I) could come to Zion.

I couldn't watch them bury her, so I stood a long way from the grave while they lowered her casket into the ground.

There had been so many big changes in my life, I couldn't bear it all. I was twenty years old, soon to have my second child, about to move hundreds of miles away from my family. I wanted to block out the memory of this dark day, but I couldn't.

Mother's sickness and death would come to haunt me in my dreams.

11

Do You Have Cows?

When Father bade us move to the lands of refuge, he told us that the gentiles and apostates (former members who had left the church) wanted to kill us, and that soon there would be a great martyrdom in the city of Short Creek. The people's only chance for survival and redemption would be to move to the lands of refuge.

The day after Mother's funeral, Father sent me with Rich back to the land of refuge in South Dakota, known as R23, where he had been living with two of his other ladies. R23 was located in a secluded area of the Black Hills just south of Pringle in the southwest corner of the state, not far from Mount Rushmore. With only three FLDS families living there, I wondered where Father would have me give birth. No one there had any midwifery experience, and this baby would be coming along in a few weeks.

Since only the worthiest people could live on the lands of refuge, Father had recorded hours of "special trainings" for the people there to listen to and live by. Every new person who came to live on the lands had to complete all of these trainings before they did anything else. If we listened from morning till night, it took about two weeks to get through them all. If anyone so much as fell asleep while listening, that person could be sent away.

There were many new rules to learn.

CLOTHING

All clothing had to be made by our own hands; none could be purchased from gentiles.

Dresses had to have shirt collars.

Dresses had to be made of light pastel colors, because God delights in pastels.

HAIR

No more braids hanging down our backs. God now wanted us to wear our hair up on our heads. A woman's hair was considered sacred and was to be used for sacred ordinances with her husband in the temple, so its length could not be revealed.

PRAYER

Women and children had to kneel down to pray in a prayer circle every hour on the hour, from five o'clock in the morning until seven o'clock at night.

To get up late or miss hourly prayer was a grievous sin before God. Missing too often would result in being sent away from the lands of refuge, and repentance and rebaptism would be required to return.

FOOD

We could eat only food we made ourselves.

Purchasing processed food was forbidden.

Sugar was forbidden.

White flour was forbidden. Only wheat flour—and eventually only wheat flour grown by our own hands—was allowed.

Milk had to be raw. Gentile homogenized milk was forbidden.

Only meat from cows and chickens raised on the lands was allowed.

There was a positive in all of these new requirements: the people learned many useful skills. We lived off the land and the work of our own hands, and I remain grateful to this day for the knowledge and ability to do that. It taught us not only self-sufficiency but also a healthy lifestyle and respect for the land. And everybody worked for the greater good of the community. The storehouse was the church store, which ran as a cooperative for the benefit of everyone. Members' labors for the church not only stocked the shelves but earned us the privilege of getting what we needed. The ladies all learned how to sew every kind of clothing for the storehouse: jeans, dresses, underwear, briefs, leggings, and bras (which we were required to call "support articles" because the word *bra* was considered evil). We learned how to process milk into cheese, yogurt, sour cream, and butter. We canned all types of fruit and vegetables. The men earned their privileges through their construction labors, as they were in charge of putting up the buildings on the lands of refuge. All members were required to donate anything that they did not need to the storehouse for others to use. The church also purchased food and other personal items that we were unable to make ourselves. No money changed hands—as a member of the United Order, we were allowed to get anything we needed, with the caveat that we must never take anything extra.

The early settlers of the lands of refuge were instructed to build homes quickly for the people who would be coming after us. Men were brought in from Short Creek without their families as "laborers of Zion" to complete the construction. There were strict deadlines for each building, and if the men did not meet them, the punishment was severe. Some men lost their families forever as a result of missing these dates. The men were given just fourteen days to build one house with fourteen bedrooms and twelve bathrooms and enormous living areas; it took sixty men working twenty-two hours a day to meet the deadline and keep their families and salvation.

The women were forbidden to help with the construction work. Our job was to take care of the gardens and the cooking and cleaning. We were forbidden to spend time with or even near the laborers, too—they slept in trailers or in their trucks. Some were allowed to stay in a room in one of the houses where no women lived. A few older ladies on the land were in charge of preparing meals for the crew.

I was in the Black Hills only two weeks when Father told Rich to take me back to Texas to stay with Father's family until my baby was born. I can only assume he had the same thought as I did about there being no midwife on the lands in South Dakota.

It was another very long ride for a very pregnant woman, but I was so glad to see my little sisters again. Amber wrapped her little arms around my legs and yelled with great excitement, "Hi, Rachel! Hi!"

"I love you," I said quietly in her ear, my heart aching for this motherless girl.

When I went inside, it hit me all over again that Mother was gone, and that I would never find refuge or solace in her room again. I was overwhelmed with a sense of loneliness. Mother Annette invited me to stay in her room with her, but she had eleven children, many of whom were still young, making her room a hot spot of wild children coming and going at all hours. It was already hard to get any rest because I was so uncomfortable when I lay down, and the added constant noise made it nearly impossible to nap or sleep through the night.

One morning I walked into the dining room and found Father flirting with several young girls I recognized from my class when I had taught third grade. They couldn't have been more than thirteen or fourteen years old now.

"What are those girls doing here?" I asked Angela.

She laughed. "They're married to Father."

"No way!" I watched as Father hugged and kissed them, essentially showing off his new little brides to the family. *I know what you're going through*, I thought. *He tricks you into thinking it is God's will.* When I couldn't stand to watch this scene any longer, I went down the hall to Angela's room; she came to join me a few minutes later.

"What's wrong?" Angela said.

"I'm a little surprised Father married such young girls." I didn't dare say too much. Talking against the Prophet was unforgivable, so our conversation pretty much stopped right there.

Over the next weeks, Father spent most of his time in his room as waves of "mothers" went in and out in groups. I tried to convince myself that whatever was happening in that room was innocent, that he was a better man now that he was the Prophet.

(What I didn't yet know was that Father had had a new revelation that he called the New Law of Sarah, which allowed him to have multiple naked wives with him at one time, all in the name of God, to give him "heavenly comfort" as he solemnly atoned for the sins of the people. This law required the women to sexually touch and excite each other as well as Father with the promise that they were all working together for Father's benefit as "God's servant." He said that these girls had been given to him by God "before they go through teenage doubting and fears and boy troubles. I will just be their boy trouble and guide them right." He especially liked to bring in young new brides who found this activity repulsive, because it aroused him to watch these girls do something they hated. My own experience began to make more sense—the more I abhorred what he made me do, the more pleasure he had gotten from it.)

A few days later, Father called the people together for a general meeting. He chastised some of the men for not completing a home they were building on time. As a result, he said he would now have to atone for the people so that God might forgive them. "I will pray for you," Father said, and we all bowed our heads. As he was praying, he began to slur, and the words he spoke sounded like nonsense. I opened my eyes and saw he was shaking violently, and then he slowly fell to the ground, unconscious.

What an excellent actor, I thought. But the people in the room bought the act: women were crying, and the men were speechless. I had an urge to laugh, but I knew if I did I would surely be damned.

Father's wife Naomi stood up. "Leave! Everyone leave!" The people filed out of the meeting house as quickly as possible.

"How could we bring this upon our Prophet? We have truly sinned," I heard someone say. The women were still crying.

I wondered if Father had really gone weird in the head. Trying to convince himself that he was the Prophet of the people went against all the rules of the church, and he knew he was a sinner. Maybe the contradiction was too much for his mind to handle?

Weeks later, Father called a special meeting. He said that God wanted some of his close wives to testify that his odd behavior during the special prayer had been his atoning for us, and that he had suffered greatly on our behalf. The wives testified that they had felt the power of God around him and had seen visions of angels surrounding him and administering to him as the spirit of God rushed over him.

Why does he have to explain it to us if it was really God? I thought. But most everyone else seemed to accept all of this as coming from God.

My little sister Josie stopped me in the dining room. "Rachel, do you have cows at the land of refuge you live at?"

Father was sitting at the end of the table. I had promised to keep everything about R23 secret and sacred. But cows? I said "Yes" quickly and walked out of the room.

The next day Father was on the move again, but he called me from the road. "The Lord showed me that you have been talking about the land where you live to your sisters and my family at R17. The Lord calls upon you to repent. Answer me honestly: What have you told about the land of refuge R23?"

I told him about Josie asking about cows, which Father obviously knew about because he'd been in the room, and then he gave me a long, strong correction about keeping everything secret and sacred. Once he was done with me, Father asked to be put on the main speaker in the living room and to summon the family together, and then he gave the whole family a correction. He said if they did not keep everything secret and sacred, he would not be able to return to the land for a long time and they would all be "destroyed by God."

Afterward, I borrowed a cell phone and called Rich. "I had forgotten about all the drama in Father's family. I don't like being here."

"Rachel, be grateful. It's an honor to be at your father's house. Be patient until I am allowed to come down to be with you."

Father returned a week later during a spate of major thunderstorms, and because of the terrible weather, a building deadline was not met. Father called a meeting to correct the people. He said if he hadn't come back when he did and intervened with the Lord through his atoning, we would all have been destroyed by the storms.

Father was continually atoning for us, now. Every bad thing we survived was because he once again atoned for us. This atonement usually happened in his room, so that his wives could give him "heavenly comfort" to keep him alive. Father said the deadline wasn't met because some of the men were sinners, citing in particular presiding elder Ernest Jessop, and his counselor, Allen Steed, and he sent the two men away forever. He said he would give their families to other men who were more worthy.

This correction scared the remaining men who were laboring for Zion. They worked even harder to meet the deadlines for fear of losing their families.

The land of refuge grew quickly as houses and gardens were built, the people working diligently to please their God and Prophet. Women and children were commanded to dig up all the cactus on the 1,800-acre property because God did not like cactus on the land, Father said. Since I was hugely pregnant, I didn't participate, but I watched as the women worked, pulling up cactus after cactus and throwing them onto mountains of prickly green corpses, only to find more growing in their place a few days later. Eventually, they managed to remove all of the cactus plants from the property.

Father told the men that God had commanded that they begin construction on a large temple, and he set more impossible deadlines. As the men failed to meet them, more of them were sent away.

My water broke three weeks early, on September 5, 2004. Grandmother Sharon was my midwife again. She was worried I would get an infection, so she put me on an old antibiotic that had been donated to her. The contractions began at 7:30 that evening. The midwife decided that I would give birth in the bedroom I had been staying in, in the bed I had been sleeping in, which I wasn't too happy about.

My labor advanced quickly this time, and within two hours I was dilated to seven centimeters. But when I hadn't advanced any further twenty minutes later, the midwife gave me 9cc of Pitocin, injecting the full dose into my left thigh. Almost instantly I fell to the floor as the medicine induced one long, continuous contraction. It felt like I was having every contraction every pregnant woman had ever had all at once. I couldn't hear or see for the pain, and I began to scream and scream.

"Rachel, stop acting like that!" Rich said, pulling me up off the floor and lifting me onto the bed. He had come back from South Dakota a week earlier. I told myself the only way to make the agony stop was to push the baby out, and I did.

My relief was instantaneous when I saw my new baby daughter.

The next day the midwife, the assistant midwife, and some of Father's wives came to see me. They asked why I had lost control during the delivery. One of them said, "Women in the priesthood do not lose control and scream like that."

I felt ashamed. I didn't know until years later that that much Pitocin all at once was the reason I wasn't able to handle the pain, and that it could have ruptured my uterus or killed my baby.

12

Land of Refuge

As soon as I was able to travel, Rich took me and our new baby back to R23. After five weeks of living at R17 with Father's family in Texas, I couldn't wait to leave. I felt bad for my brothers and sisters who had to live there amid all that stress and the fear of being sent away over even the smallest infraction.

But distance hardly took us out from under Father's thumb. When he named my second daughter Martha, I said to Rich, "I wish so much that we could name our own babies. Father gives them ugly, grandmotherly names." (Rich's mother's name was Martha.)

"Don't say that, Rachel. It's a privilege to have your father name our children. He is inspired by Heavenly Father, and you should feel grateful."

Thanks to the antibiotic the midwife had given me, I developed a serious yeast infection called thrush, which caused my nipples to swell painfully and bleed, so it became difficult to nurse my newborn. Medical intervention wasn't an option, since we were supposed to keep ourselves hidden from the outside world, and Father said doctors were reserved for life-and-death situations only (and even then, as he'd proved with my mother's illness, he might not allow it). Instead, we were to pray to God for healing.

Rich was glad that I couldn't nurse, because Father had given the men "celestial morals" training back in February, during which he told them that they must never have sex with a wife who was pregnant or nursing. Rich encouraged me to bottle-feed Martha.

My infection lasted for several months, until Rich asked one of the men who was going to Short Creek to pick up some Diflucan from one of the certified nurses that worked at the Hildale Health Center. The Diflucan took care of the infection, but I was never able to nurse my baby again, because by then I had lost my milk.

Our family was living in an apartment in the storehouse with a single small kitchen/dining area, a small living room, and four bedrooms. Rich put me in the room next to his, and Susan and Molly both had their own rooms. Trish was still in Short Creek, but we had her two girls with us, which meant all of the wives had two or more children sharing our bedrooms.

My sister wives grew increasingly jealous. They thought that, since I wasn't nursing, Rich and I were having sex every time we were alone together. Accordingly, they came up with creative ways to take their jealousy out on me and my children. Sometimes Rich had me go with him on errands that Father sent him on, and he would tell me to leave Barbie, who was not yet two years old, at home. When I returned, I'd see that she had been left to take care of herself during my absence. She had to dress herself and figure out how to clean herself when she soiled her pants. The evidence was plain: she looked disheveled, and my bathroom and bedroom were a mess.

I was furious, but there was nothing I could do about it. Rich would just tell me, "Just love and forgive your sister wives. That's the only way to help Barbie."

When we weren't vying for Rich's attention, all of us ladies learned a lot about survival during those first years in South

Dakota. Our water had to be hauled in from a distant town, and there were times the water truck broke down and we went without water for up to two days. In winter, we would gather snow in pans and melt it to have water to clean and cook. It made me realize how ungrateful I had always been for the luxury of running water.

The four of us spent a lot of time sewing clothing for our family. At first everything looked pretty terrible and amateurish, but eventually we learned to sew fast and well. We even had some fun while we did it, as long as Rich wasn't around to make everyone jealous.

Rich was in charge of the storehouse, and he had me manage the inventory records and the accounting. I taught myself how to use QuickBooks to keep track of everything. Rich also assigned me to the greenhouse, where I planted seeds and raised the starter plants of fruits, flowers, and vegetables for our garden. I didn't know much about it, but I learned through trial and error and from whatever books I could find on the subject.

My sister wife Molly milked the cows and tended the chickens. She often took the children with her to help with feedings and other chores with the animals, which they really enjoyed.

That turned out to be a blessing, because in early 2005, Father sent us a revelation that the Lord did not want the children to have toys of any kind. He said that God considered dolls a mockery of his image and an idol. Bikes, skates, games—anything fun or entertaining—was deemed of the devil.

Rich instructed us to burn the toys we had, making the children all put their own toys in the fire barrel. Rich tried to make them feel like it was an honor to burn their toys to fulfill Heavenly Father's will as they threw handfuls of blocks, books, and dolls of all kinds in. But when Rich told Barbie to throw in the little doll her late grandmother had given her, she was inconsolable. I wanted to take her in my arms and comfort her, but Rich was right there, encouraging her that she was doing the will of Heavenly Father.

Father next sent word that any music that we had not composed ourselves was forbidden and must be burned. This directive was hard on me in particular because I loved all kinds of music. Our family sings on Sunday evenings had been a lovely memory from childhood, and we had always had a piano in the house. I knew how to play a lot of gentile songs on the violin and piano, too, but now I could no longer play them. It took me several months to bring myself to burn my music; in fact, I secretly kept some of my favorite recordings and sheet music, but I never played them for fear someone would tell on me if they heard.

Work was the only thing left for any of us to do, and there was plenty of that just making sure we had what we needed, including medicine. We grew all the herbs we could in the South Dakota climate. When the children got sick, we made them herbal teas and figured out natural medicines to heal them. One day, I had left my daughters with my sister Melanie, who was now living there, while I went to general meeting. Melanie burst into the room in the middle of the meeting, carrying a wailing Martha. My sister had fallen asleep while little Martha was jumping on the bed. She had jumped clear off the bed and landed on a space heater, and her foot got stuck. Melanie woke up when she heard Martha's screams.

I grabbed my daughter and ran to the bathroom to put her foot under cold water. I watched the skin fall off her little ankle and the bottom of her foot.

Melanie felt terrible and helped me tend to Martha. I made an herbal poultice for her ankle and foot, changing it every five hours. Luckily, Martha was walking again in two days, and her burns healed so well there was very little scarring, although she permanently lost the feeling in some spots because the nerve endings were burned so badly.

Most women in the church started out with another baby when their youngest was around a year old. But after Martha, I wasn't able to get pregnant, which made the sister wives even more jealous, and more inclined to believe Rich and I were having sex all the time. (We weren't.) I grew desperate to get pregnant, if only because I didn't like everyone being mad at me. The wives were all angry at Rich too, and he began to spend less and less time with me to appease them.

Baby Martha was a happy and laughing child, which earned her the favor of everyone who spent time with her. Rich adored her and doted on her, but that made her a target for the other ladies. Rich had me make the cheese for the storehouse every day from the milk we got from our cows, and he didn't let me bring my girls with me, which meant I had to leave them at home. My sister wives would put Martha down for a nap at 10:00 a.m. or earlier inside my dark closet, with the door closed. Often when I got home at two or three in the afternoon, I would find her still there, because she was unable to open the door.

Meanwhile, trouble was heating up for Father.

In June 2005 the authorities finally made their move against him. A grand jury in Mohave County, Arizona, indicted him for sexual misconduct with a minor, for conspiracy to commit sexual misconduct with a minor, and for arranging a plural marriage between a teenage girl and an older man. That same month, federal prosecutors charged him with unlawful flight to avoid prosecution. The Utah attorney general asked a judge to freeze the church's assets, which amounted to more than $100 million. For years the church had owned and operated a number of construction, machining, and other commercial businesses that had brought in enormous sums of money that were used to fund the purchase and building of the various lands of refuge and other church properties. In July, Utah and Arizona got together to jointly announce a $10,000 reward for information leading to Father's arrest.

In November Father's younger brother, Seth, was pulled over in Colorado with more than $140,000 in cash, prepaid phone cards and credit cards, and stacks of letters addressed to Father either as "Warren Jeffs" or "The Prophet." Seth admitted to the authorities that he was bringing these things to Father, but he refused to give them Father's location.

Rich married his fifth wife, Gloria, in December 2005. Gloria, chosen for Rich by Father, had just turned sixteen when she arrived in South Dakota. Trish was finally deemed worthy to join us from Short Creek as well.

With the additional people, we could no longer fit in the storehouse apartment, so Father told Rich to move our family into one of the apartments in the new duplex, a large three-story log cabin divided into two separate living spaces. We had the south apartment, and another family occupied the north. The top floor of the duplex had four bedrooms and two bathrooms; the middle floor had a good-size kitchen, dining area, and living room; and the bottom floor had three more bedrooms and a laundry room.

Father had personally designed all the houses on the lands of refuge, and they were all very well built. He had instructed the men doing the work that everything should be plain—plain carpet in light colors and white walls. Large closets were a must, so that family members could kneel for prayers in them; we were continually taught to supplicate God in our secret places. The furniture was all handmade and very high quality—dressers, tables, chairs, and beds. The women assisted in making the upholstery for the couches and chairs, and sewing fabric for curtains. The result was far better than anything you could buy in a gentile store.

Rich's family was experiencing growing pains. With each new wife came a new source of jealousy and resentment. The other ladies had been treating our newest sister wife, Gloria, badly, which made her seek out my friendship. But if the other ladies were mad at me, they would be friendly with Gloria and tell her what they were doing to me or my kids behind my back. Then Gloria would come and tell me.

Complaining to Rich about my sister wives got me nowhere. And that year, while I couldn't get pregnant, things got worse and worse. The other women went so far as to try to turn Rich against me—I would often wake up in the morning to find my door had been locked in the night so Rich couldn't get in my room. Once, Rich lost the keys to his truck. When he asked me if I knew where they were, I said, honestly, "No, I don't." Molly then told Rich that she'd seen me take them and he should check my drawer, where he found the keys. (Susan told me later that Molly had put them there.)

When I finally did get pregnant, I miscarried. I asked Rich to come talk to me in my room so I could tell him what happened. "I will have to sneak through your window so that the ladies don't know I'm talking to you," Rich said. I was livid. *I did not choose to marry you*, I thought, *and yet I am your wife, and I should be treated as much like a wife as any of the others*. I knew I couldn't say what I was thinking, or he would treat me even worse.

Father came to visit us in South Dakota in May 2006, around

the same time the US attorney general charged him with unlawful flight, and the FBI added him to its Ten Most Wanted list, offering a reward of $100,000 for information leading to his capture.

Father told us none of this, and since we had no access to television or radio, we had no way of knowing. Instead, he told us all to write letters of confession, naming our sins to him. In my letter, I told him that I was angry at my sister wives for how they treated me and my children. Father, who was now wanted by the federal government alongside murderers and drug traffickers, sent me a message of correction that said I was unworthy to see him and that our whole family had sinned.

Our punishment would be stark.

13

This Is What Hell Feels Like

Father commanded that all of us—except Rich and his newest wife, Gloria—must now go live in a house of hiding in Las Vegas until we were worthy to go back to the lands of refuge.

And so four women and twelve children, all under school age, moved in with Rich's brother Robert and his wife Cynthia in a small home in the middle of a city famous for its abundance of vice. There were four bedrooms; Robert and Cynthia had the largest, and the rest of us shared the other three. In the name of making us wives get along, Rich put Molly and me with my girls in one room, Susan and Trish in another room with the boys, and all the other girls in the third.

The yard was even smaller than the house, but it didn't really matter because we had been told to stay inside and out of sight. In our church dresses, we would stand out, and Father insisted that no one could know we were there. It seemed odd that Father would have us live in what he considered the wickedest city in the world, but I know that he believed no one would find us there. (As though anyone was looking.)

One exception to our seclusion came on the Fourth of July. I will say one thing for Las Vegas, they know how to put on a fireworks show. There was a big park behind our house, and that night, not long after we arrived, we stood in the backyard and watched an amazing display. It was the first time the children had seen fireworks at all, and they were concurrently terrified and in awe. Some of them cried in fear, but most of them thoroughly enjoyed it, exclaiming their *ooh*s and *aah*s simultaneously.

Day to day, we were all crammed into that small space with nothing to do besides prepare meals and clean. There were no toys or books for the children. We had no garden, or animals, to tend. We sister wives hated one another and were forced into closer proximity than ever. There was nowhere to escape to. The only peaceful place was the bathroom, but only for a moment, because it was never long before a child was banging on the door.

Eventually Robert got us some fabric so we could sew, but the children still had nothing but their little imaginations, which they exercised creatively in games of make-believe. We weren't supposed to let them do that, but we mothers agreed that they needed to have something to occupy their time. So they turned pillows into dolls, dressing them in the babies' clothes and pretending they were their own babies; they made houses out of couch cushions, or rode the cushions like they were horses. Whatever they wanted to use, we let them—dishes, tables, chairs, rags, you name it. Molly made some wooden blocks for them, too, and they also tried their tiny hands at cooking and sewing to stay busy. In time, we got a printer, and we printed pictures for the children to color and made our own books for them as well.

Shortly after we arrived, Rich asked Father for permission to have the children see a dentist for a checkup. Since we mothers had no access to a vehicle, Robert took the children to their first ever dental appointment. The dentist, who was a member of the church, was a generous man. He knew the rules about no toys, so he gave the children some of his actual tools and surgical masks so they could play dentist at home, which was a great thrill for them. They used upended tables for exam chairs, and blew up latex medical gloves to serve as balloons.

Trapped in this prison with these ladies who had made my life so miserable for years, I made the decision that I was going to find out if love really did conquer all. I decided that I was going to *make* myself feel love for each and every one of my sister wives, no matter what they did to me or my children. I began to do things for them even when I didn't feel like it. I'd wash dishes for them when it was their turn, or offer to cook when it was their turn to make the meal. The more I made it a point to help them and give to them out of the goodness of my heart, the more they started to love and trust me. Sometimes at night after the children were in bed, my sister wives and I would sneak over the fence in the dark and peek into other people's yards, just for something to do. Occasionally we would sit on the fence and watch our neighbor's TV through the windows, trying to guess what the people on the screen were saying.

As our bond grew, the ladies started to confess some of the things they had done to me and my girls when we were in South Dakota, things that I didn't already know about. I knew they hadn't treated my girls nicely, but I didn't know that when I wasn't home, they wouldn't let my little girls, who were one and two at the time, go upstairs. The other children had free run of the house, but my two little ones were forced to stay in my bedroom downstairs. My girls received harsh spankings, and the other children were allowed to be mean to them. The ladies admitted to going through the garbage in my bathroom to see if I was on my period or had taken a pregnancy test, to determine if I was having sex with Rich. They'd even looked for bloody evidence that I had really miscarried.

We had just one phone between us, and usually one wife would keep it in case Rich called. The only person we could talk to on it was Rich, and depending on which wife had the phone when he called, he would struggle to convince her to let him speak to me. I got used to going long periods without speaking with him. I made a conscious decision that it wasn't going to be a big deal to me if I talked to him or not. Of course I wanted his love, but if he wanted affection from me, he would have to work for it. I was done feeling like a teenager trying to get his attention. Eventually, Rich told us that each of the ladies were to take turns keeping the phone for a week.

On August 28, after we had been in Las Vegas for about two months, Rich called and asked to speak to all of us on speaker. The four of us went into the room Trish and Susan shared, so we could hear him away from the noise of all the children.

"Uncle Warren has been arrested," Rich said.

For a moment, it was like the vacuum that comes right after an enormous explosion and sucks up all the air.

We had known for a couple of years that the world was out to get Father, and that's why he was on the road so much. But Father had also told us many times that God would protect him so that he could perform the work of the Lord. Just about everyone in the church was certain he couldn't be caught.

When Father was caught, it was via a simple traffic stop outside Vegas, not that far from our house of hiding. A trooper from the Nevada Department of Public Safety pulled over the SUV he was riding in for having paper license plates instead of proper metal ones. In the car with him were Uncle Isaac, who was driving, and Mother Naomi. Father was in the back seat. At first Father lied about who he was, but the trooper, Eddie Dutchover, recognized Father from his Wanted poster, and Father was taken to the Clark County Detention Center and held without bail pending extradition to either Arizona or Utah. (The cops let Isaac and Naomi go.)

"You ladies must pray for the Prophet's deliverance," Rich said.

Father had taught the people that if the Prophet was persecuted, it proved that ours was the true church. The world didn't like our religion, but then, the world was wicked. The state of Utah had changed the age of consent for marriage specifically so they could put Father in prison, we were told—not just by Father but by the people around him. That was how he rallied the people to help him when he was on the run, and how he kept the people faithful after he was put in jail.

But I knew better. *Now he will be punished for his sins*, I thought. I knew he hadn't been arrested because of what he'd done to me, but it still seemed like God was punishing him for it. And yet, I felt a little bit sorry for him that he was in jail.

And then it hit me.

With Father locked up, we were never going to get out of Las Vegas.

The church came to a standstill. The people were used to being told what to do in every aspect of their lives, and many would do nothing until Father gave instructions.

I prayed. Even though my faith in my father as God's servant on earth had wavered, I prayed to God as my personal friend. It was comforting to my soul, and I believed that somehow, some way, God would cause Father to communicate to Rich and tell him to get his family out of this house of hiding. Even if Father had done wrong, and even if Father didn't really talk to God or receive His word, I believed God could at least make Father want to send me back to South Dakota. Rich wasn't going to do anything until Father told him to, however—that was clear.

I yearned for a time when the children could run around out in the sunshine again, or feel rain on their faces, or see a rainbow in the sky, or watch a bug crawl through the grass. It was unhealthy for them to be stuck inside that little house all day. Every once in a while, one or two of the children would sneak out into the yard, but Robert or Cynthia would inevitably hear them through the window and yell at them to come back inside.

That fall, Rich asked his brother David to allow me to use his Clavinova piano, because Rich wanted me to learn to compose my own music for the family. He knew we were stuck in a house with a dozen bored preschoolers. I was so grateful to have something to do that I enjoyed. Learning to compose was challenging, but it was fun to make up the songs and teach them to the children. By Rich's birthday in January, I had a full program of songs for the children to sing for him, which I recorded and sent to him.

As winter came and flu season arrived, the children got sick often, and so did the adults. In such tight quarters, we passed around the same bugs over and over. We figured out natural home remedies to see us through: onions, garlic, and citrus fruit were essential.

It crossed my mind that Father had more freedom in actual prison than we did in this prison he'd put us in. I grew to hate Las Vegas, and I vowed never to let myself get angry or upset again so that I would never be punished like this again. I learned to value patience—patience to endure and survive in difficult situations. Patience was strength.

I recognized my own weakness, so that I could be kinder and more forgiving to those I felt had hurt me. It was the one positive that came out of this trial.

In January 2007 Father, who had been extradited to Utah to await trial on two counts of rape by accomplice, confessed to several family members by phone and in video recordings that he was a wicked man and not the Prophet. Father's brothers and wives did not believe him. They were convinced that he had been drugged at the prison, because the Prophet would never say such things.

A few days later Father tried to kill himself, first by hanging himself in his cell, then by slamming his head against the cell wall. We didn't know these things at the time. All we were told was that he was suffering, and I admit, my heart ached a little when I heard. Even after everything he had done to me, even though I knew he had done wicked things, he was still my father, and I had loved him, and I believed he loved me, at least to a degree.

The prison doctors treated him for depression, and a few weeks later, when he felt better, he took back everything he had confessed. It had just been a spiritual test, Father said.

Uncle Nephi managed Father's communication with members of the family, arranging phone calls and visits at the prison. Even behind bars, Father was still very much in charge, using his brothers to do his bidding. In April 2007 Nephi relayed a message to Rich that he should drive down from South Dakota to R17 in Texas so Father could speak to him. (Father's phone privileges were limited to just a few numbers.)

Afterward, Rich called us from the road. He was on his way to Las Vegas. "The Prophet wants me to get the children," he said.

For some reason, I had a feeling that wasn't the whole story.

Rich called back a few hours later to speak to me. "Rachel, I'm going to get you too. Are you surprised?"

"I knew I was coming with you."

"How?"

"I just did."

Father had actually instructed Rich to bring me and one other wife whom Rich felt had repented, and he chose Molly. The other ladies would stay behind by themselves.

Rich was elated to be bringing most of his family home, but we had one problem: he had come with only a Ford pickup truck with a camper shell over the bed to carry back two women and twelve children who then ranged in age from one to six. Rich told the children to get in the back, and he had Molly and me take turns sitting with him in front.

The weather was stormy during the entire trip. It snowed so hard in Wyoming that Rich had trouble seeing the road in front of him, and at one point the truck slid clear off the highway and into a snowbank on the shoulder. Rich tried repeatedly to get the truck back on the road, but the wheels spun uselessly, sinking farther and farther into snow. We were stuck.

"Rachel, get in back with the children and tell them they must be silent. We could get in a lot of trouble if someone finds out they're back there." There wasn't a child seat or safety belt to be had in the bed of that truck.

As I squeezed through the back window, I thought, *This is a bad idea*. But I knew I had to obey my husband without question because he was my priesthood head, the man who is head of the household. (Before I was married, Father was my priesthood head.)

"Lie down," I said to the children. "We have to be very quiet." I pulled all the blankets we had in the truck over them and told them to snuggle close together for warmth. After a while, I heard a police car pull up and an officer giving Rich instructions through the driver's-side window. The children shivered silently, half with cold and half with fear of being discovered.

Twenty minutes later, my muscles began to cramp from the cold. I tried to gather the children in even closer. Some of them needed to use the bathroom, and most of them were now shivering violently. I didn't know how much longer we'd be able to keep this up.

It took Rich and the policeman more than an hour to get the truck out of the snow. When we were back on the road, I stuck my head through the back window.

"I know we can't all fit in the cab, but the children have to get warm."

Rich allowed all the children to squish into the cab with the adults to warm up. It took us more than twenty hours to get to South Dakota—a fifteen-hour drive in good weather—because of the storms. But after nearly a year in the house of hiding in Las Vegas, I was so grateful to be heading back to where the children had room to live and play in the sunshine again.

14

The Good Years

"Richard wants you in our room," Gloria said to me the second night after we got back to South Dakota.

Things had changed at R23 since we'd been gone. Rich had lived alone with his youngest wife Gloria the whole time, and now they had a baby. They were sharing a home with another family, which now left us with a total of three rooms for twelve children and four adults. Rich had Molly take half the children in one room with her, the other half with me in another room. Rich and Gloria shared a room with their baby, which meant he had to let Gloria know when he wanted to sleep with one of his other ladies—hence "*our*" room." That was hard for her after having him to herself for so long.

My first thought was, *Sorry, Gloria, we have as much right to him as you do*. I did understand how she felt, though I struggled with the fact that she shared a room with our husband. None of the other ladies had ever gotten to share a room with Rich full-time.

I went to my husband with a different way of thinking than I'd had before my time away from him. I would always be kind and receptive to him when he called for me, but I was done letting his decisions run my emotions. Just as I had decided not to fight with my sister wives anymore to save my own sanity, I now resolved that I would not fight for Rich's attention—I would not seek him out as I had in the past. From now on, he would have to be the one to come to me; he would have to make the effort to win my love.

I was going to be a lot more careful about what I said to Rich, as well. Before Vegas, I had treated him like my best friend and closest confidant, openly expressing how I felt, whether I was angry or jealous or upset about something one of my sister wives had done. Looking back on it, I realized that had always gotten me into trouble. It is what got us all sent away. It took me a long time to learn that lesson, but that year in Vegas had matured me. I wouldn't indulge those feelings anymore, but if I did have them, I sure wasn't going to tell him.

Still, it was hard to quell the jealousy that reared up in my heart when Rich slept with another wife. It was hard to get past the sense of betrayal. How could a man profess his love for one wife, then happily take another into his bed the next day? I had to remind myself that none of us chose this situation. Rich did not choose his wives, and we did not choose him. All I could do instead was try to appreciate the fact that Rich loved all of his family.

Within a month we had moved into the duplex again, having a full apartment for our family, and when Trish and Susan returned to South Dakota a few months after we did, the family was finally whole again. The ladies were so happy to see their children, and the children were delighted to have their mothers back. We all seemed to get along better since our experience in Vegas. We all shared everything: our home, our food, and our children. Rich made a family schedule every week, with the wives taking turns making meals, cleaning the house, and tending the children. This equal division of labor had the added benefit of making the children less selfish and more sociable because they dealt with so many people on a continual basis.

As a result, the next few years were the happiest of my married life.

"Who wants to help me feed the cows?" Rich asked the children after breakfast. He was an extremely kind and loving father, and made an effort to do things with them whenever he could.

"I do!" the children said in unison.

"Hurry and help do the breakfast dishes, then you can come with me." The children rushed around clearing off the tables, wiping down high chairs, and sweeping floors while Rich hooked the trailer to the four-wheeler.

When the children finished their chores, they ran outside to join their father. Rich had made benches for the trailer for them to sit on. I was pregnant again, so I stayed behind to look after Rich and Gloria's baby, Shirley, so that Gloria could go along to help tend the children.

After Rich had finished the animal chores with the children, he brought Martha down to my room for her nap. He lay on my bed next to her and asked her to sing a song to him. She launched into the hymn "Angry Words," but she didn't know all the words—"from the tongue unbridled slip" is a mouthful for a toddler—and her effort to sing the song was the cutest thing ever.

"Come here, Mother Rachel," Rich said, patting the bed next to them. I went over and sat down. Rich took Martha's little hand and placed it on my growing tummy. "Do you feel that, Martha? Mother is going to have a new little baby." Martha laughed in delight as the baby's foot kicked her little hand. Barbie, who had been lying on her own bed, came over to feel it too. The girls could not wait to meet their new sibling.

I spent the last few months of 2007 getting bigger and composing music for everyone to sing on Rich's birthday in January.

It had been a hit with Rich last year, and this year we would be in the same place with Rich, so we could sing it to him in person. The sister wives had agreed to make all the girl children matching green dresses for the birthday program, and we shared the sewing workload among us.

Susan taught school for all of the older children in a small shed outside our house; I taught preschool and kindergarten. During recess, I gathered all the children together to rehearse our birthday songs. I think the children enjoyed this special time we shared as much as I did.

Father was kinder that year, as well. Maybe being locked up in the Purgatory Correctional Facility (yes, it's really called that), thirty miles northwest of Short Creek in southern Utah, had chastened him or softened his heart. Father still sent the people messages from prison, passed along through phone calls or letters, and the people still followed his word. He sent several messages for "my handmaid Rachel," asking for my forgiveness again. Other times he sent stern messages of correction, but he was generally less strict than he had been. He may have been somewhat distracted by the preparations for his trial on charges of rape as an accomplice, which began on September 10, 2007.

The star witness was Elissa Wall, who had been married at the age of fourteen to Allen Steed—Steed was her first cousin, and nineteen years old at the time. Father had performed the wedding at the same motel in Caliente where I was married. Making a perfect snapshot of what living in the church was like, Allen Steed testified in Father's defense. When Steed was asked by the prosecutor, "If you were told by the Prophet to disobey the laws of man, would you do it?" he said, "I would." Steed was later charged with felony rape, but a plea deal resulted in a lesser charge of "solemnizing a prohibited marriage" and just a month in jail.

Father was convicted on both counts, and two months later the judge sentenced him to two consecutive sentences of five years to life in prison. He still faced charges in Arizona as well as federal charges of unlawful flight.

Being a convicted felon did nothing to lessen Father's position as leader of the church—in fact, he was still controlling every aspect of the people's lives.

In January he sent a message that he wanted me to go to the land of refuge in Texas to stay with his family while I waited to have my baby, since there was a midwife there. I was due February 29, although I had already decided I wasn't giving birth on Leap Day, because I wanted my child to have a real birthday.

Rich drove me down and returned to the family in the Black Hills of South Dakota, but I didn't mind that he had to go back, I was so happy to see my brothers and sisters again. I hadn't seen them since the summer of 2005. There had been a lot of construction since the last time I was there, with many new homes, and the new temple was now finished.

That night I lay on my sister Angela's bed with her while she told me what had been happening during the last couple of years, since I had not been allowed any contact with them. Father had ordered that there be no communication between the different lands of refuge, since everything at all times was a secret. You could only know what happened on any particular land of refuge if you lived there, which is why I had gotten in trouble for telling my little sister that we had cows in South Dakota.

Angela and I stayed up all night. She told me that before Father was caught by the authorities, he had married off our sister Teresa the day after she turned fifteen to Angela's husband, Raymond Jessop, who was also married to my sister Maryanne, as well as two of my cousins, two of my aunts, and two Musser girls, Mary and Marie. So Teresa had to negotiate life as a plural wife—Ray's ninth—at such a young age. At first I was surprised, since Father had allowed his other daughters to wait until they were eighteen, or at least very close to eighteen. But it made more sense when I remembered those little girls Father had married himself.

Then, three months after Father was arrested, he had Raymond Jessop sent away from his family, which meant my sisters had no husband, so Father had all three move back in with his family. Angela had to have her baby without her husband, and the stress of that caused complications during the birth at home. She ended up having a C-section in the hospital to save her life and the baby's.

"I'm really sad that all this happened to you," I said. "But I'm glad I get to spend some time with you now."

We both told stories of our sister-wife struggles, and Angela told me how hard her married life had been. Like me, she had been on the receiving end of her sister wives' jealousy, because they thought their husband, Ray, loved her the most. Despite how hard it was to hear certain things, it was also fun and comforting to be able to pour my heart out to Angela and share the thoughts and feelings I'd kept hidden deep within me all this time.

The next few weeks were happy ones for me; I spent lots of time with my other sisters, and gossiped and laughed late into the night. Mother Annette came into our room one night, acting like she was sleepwalking. She held her hands out in front of her and walked in an unstable, crazy manner, just to make the girls scream. Then she laughed and said, "You girls go to bed!"

One day I was taking a walk with Angela when we ran into Tina Steed, an old friend of mine, on a dirt road. Tina showed off her two beautiful children, a boy around two years old and a baby daughter. She told me that when her son was just a few weeks old, Father had told her she was unworthy and made her leave the lands of refuge to repent, leaving her baby behind. How could he separate a tiny, helpless baby from his mother like that? Father had let her return after her son was a year old.

All of Father's family took time out of their days to come see me. I had missed them all so much. I spent most of my time sewing with Teresa and Josie. Josie had kept most of Mother's belongings, so we went through it all together. Josie wanted me to take a lot of it, but the memory of Mother was still hard on me because of all that she'd gone through with her illness and being separated from her children. It hurt too much to think about it, so I didn't want to take anything that would remind me.

Even though Teresa was married, once she went back to live in Father's house, everyone treated her like a child. She wasn't allowed to make her own choices or be responsible for herself. Both she and Angela still loved Ray, and they missed him. Maryanne missed him some, but had had a lot of struggles with jealousy and didn't know if she wanted to go back to him. In fact, her struggle with jealousy over Ray's spending time with his other wives was the reason Father had sent him away. It was all a big mess.

I got to spend time with my brothers during their mealtimes too. They were required to eat downstairs, away from Father's wives and daughters, so that they would not be tempted to look at or like the girls. The boys shared bedrooms down one hall, and the girls down another, and each group was prohibited from entering the other's area. Married sisters were allowed to talk to the brothers as long as we didn't get caught doing it too often.

Rich came down to Texas to be with me a week before my due date, bringing my two little girls with him. Father's family were so happy to see them, and everyone was intent on spoiling them every chance they got. I was glad to have my husband and daughters with me.

I had asked the midwife if there was any way to induce labor before February 29. She gave me Cytotec and several other drugs, but nothing worked. And then, wouldn't you know, at four o'clock in the morning on Leap Day, I had my first contraction. God was reminding me that He was in charge, not me.

"I guess what I want doesn't really matter, because we're having a Leap baby," I said to Rich.

I figured that if this baby was like the first two, it wouldn't come out until I was almost dead from pushing. In the end, the labor was a little easier than it had been with Martha, but even so I was very glad when it was all over. My new baby son weighed eight and a half pounds, and he was perfect.

Father had sent a message with instructions what to name the baby. I had really hoped I'd be able to name this child, especially since Father was in prison, but Rich was as loyal to Father as ever. Rulon it was.

All of Father's large family wanted to meet the new baby. There had been some bad viruses going around that winter, so the midwife did her darnedest to keep the sick children away from the baby, but with so many people and little ones coming and going, she wasn't entirely successful.

Rich wanted us to head back to South Dakota a few days after

Me, all smiles at four years old.

ABOVE: Jeffs family portrait, 1992, the year Father started summoning me to his office alone. I am the girl on the right with my hands on my cheeks, pretending to be cute. I was eight years old.

Father and I, when I was twelve, about the same age as some of his later wives.

ABOVE LEFT: My sister Becky and I at eighteen, the year Father married us to brothers Richard and David Allred, who worked as guards for Grandfather when he was the Prophet. ABOVE RIGHT: With my husband, Rich. I was the third of his five wives. I didn't love him when we were first married—I only met him the day before our wedding—but I grew to love him over time.

With three of my sister wives. The church teaches that it is good for a man to have multiple wives, and that jealousy is a grievous sin. But even though I grew up in polygamy, once it became my reality as a sister wife, I learned how hard it was.

Three generations: my mother shortly after her cancer diagnosis, me (in the wedding dress Mother Ora made for me), and my baby girl Barbie. Mother wanted some nice pictures with us before she lost her hair to chemo. Father sent Mother's younger children away when she got sick; he said her cancer was proof that she wasn't worthy.

Most of my sisters in South Dakota. Father had relocated his family there after the 2008 raid on the Land of Refuge in Texas.

Father sent me and my sisters away from our children to a house of hiding in Idaho. To stay sane, we had to do some crazy things.

Father sent Rich and me away from our children to repent when I was still nursing my youngest: my son Nathaniel trying to squirm away from me after I returned. He didn't remember me.

In 2012, Father sent me away yet again, this time to a house of hiding in Colorado with my sister Becky, falsely accusing us of murdering unborn children. We were forbidden contact with anyone but the person who dropped off food once a week. At the same time, one of my sister wives was expelled from the church altogether and my husband had to tell her children that they would never see their mother again.

Back in South Dakota with my kids at Father's house, 2013, before he sent me away from them again, this time for more than six months. For me, that was the last straw; I knew I had to leave.

Brandon and I.

My children and I, 2017.

the birth. Before we left, I went looking for my sister Angela in her room.

"I'm going to keep your phone number, just in case I need it," I told her. "And you keep mine, just in case you need it." It was a direct violation of Father's orders, but I think we'd both been through enough at Father's hands, being separated from our families, that we were willing to risk it.

"Okay, let's," Angela said. "But we can't let anyone know."

"At least text me some, okay?"

"Okay, if I dare."

We were back home for less than a week when baby Rulon developed pneumonia.

A nurse on the land had some medical supplies, including an oximeter to measure the baby's blood oxygen levels, which hovered in the mid- to upper seventies as he struggled to breathe. The nurse kept him on oxygen in an effort to raise the saturation closer to 100, where it should be. She also managed to get her hands on ceftriaxone, an antibiotic, which she injected into his leg. It was wrenching to see my newborn suffer so. As the days passed, his condition deteriorated and his weight dropped.

"Please, can we take him to the hospital?" I asked Rich several times. "He needs a doctor."

"Rachel, you know that we have been instructed to give the children a blessing and do all we can at home. Let's keep working with him here."

The antibiotic didn't seem to be helping, which made me think it may have expired. The nurse agreed, and stopped giving him the injections. I would have to rely on my own knowledge of natural healing to help him. I breastfed him as much as possible, kept him near a humidifier at all times, placed warm onion packs on his chest, and gave him drops of garlic oil. Over the next two weeks, baby Rulon slowly improved. My spirits soared when I knew that my son would be okay.

And then on the evening of April 3, I heard the family phone beep as I was walking through the living room. It was a text from my brother Ammon. I nearly dropped the phone when I saw the photos he'd sent.

I wrapped Rulon in a warm blanket and ran to the watchtower to find Rich.

15

The Raid

"Hey, you! Good morning!" Rich pulled me onto his lap and kissed my cheek. "Let me see my little man." Rich uncovered baby Rulon's face and started cooing at him.

I dug the phone out of my pocket and held it up. "Look at this. It's from Ammon."

Rich took the phone and scrolled through the photos of police cars and men in SWAT gear and camouflage, their weapons out, at the gate to R17.

"This looks bad," Rich said, and immediately dialed Merril Jessop, the bishop there. "Is everything okay?" Rich asked.

"We are surrounded by police and Texas Rangers," Merril said. "We're trying to find out what they want." Merril got off the phone quickly.

"That's it?" I said.

"He has his hands full, sounds like. I'll find out more as soon as I can."

"Rich . . . my family."

"There's nothing we can do from here, Rachel. They'll need our prayers," Rich said. "Go tell the family to pray for the people in Texas."

My heart hurt as I thought of all my family members. I loved them all so much. I walked back to the house to tell the others what was happening.

All day we waited for word, but nobody called. Around 10:00 p.m., I took the family phone down to my room and secretly texted my sister Angela. I couldn't bear not knowing what was going on.

"Are you okay?"

"We are all in a big cement building with hundreds of cots, trying to get the children to sleep," Angela wrote.

"Why are they doing this?"

"I don't know, but I can't let them know I have this phone. I'll call you when I get a chance."

A few minutes later, Ammon called. "I'm hiding in a shower stall," he said in a muffled tone.

"I'm so glad you called! I've been so worried about everyone."

"They said that they got a call from an underage girl named Sarah Jessop Barlow, saying she was married and had a baby," Ammon said. "But there is no Sarah Jessop Barlow on the land, so we know they aren't telling us the truth. I'm sure it was just an excuse to get on the land and find out what we are doing here."

By the time the investigation found the caller and discovered it was a hoax—perpetrated by a thirty-three-year-old woman named Rozita Swinton in Colorado—the wheels of so-called justice had already been set in motion. The person who had taken the call passed it to the county sheriff's office, which in turn led to a judge signing a warrant for Sarah Jessop Barlow and her husband, her alleged abuser. That's what brought the law to the doors of R17. Merril told the officers there was no such person as Sarah Jessop Barlow there. Nonetheless, he had no choice but to let Child Protective Services (CPS) caseworkers interview some of the girls.

Ammon told me the CPS workers had first gathered up all the high-school-age girls at the school and questioned them each individually. Father had been so strict in teaching the people to keep our lives on the lands of refuge secret, some of the girls wouldn't reveal how old they were or even their last names, but most of them did, and proved it with their birth certificates. The authorities were suspicious, so they decided to immediately remove some of the girls from the land, which they referred to as the YFZ Ranch.

The next day the CPS supervisor on site decided to remove all of the children, more than four hundred of them in total, saying that their mothers could come if they wanted to. Of course they wanted to protect their children, and more than 130 women voluntarily went along. Father's underage wives had been sent to their own fathers' homes so CPS wouldn't know they were married to him, but they were rounded up that night as well. The women and children—more than five hundred people—were sent to several different facilities in Eldorado and San Angelo.

At the civic center in Eldorado, where my siblings were, the mothers and older children were having trouble getting the younger children to settle down and go to sleep that first night because there were so many of them squeezed into the one building, and it was very cold inside. The mothers asked the officers to turn off the air conditioning, but their request was denied.

Over the next few days, Teresa, Josephine, Angela, and Ammon took turns calling me late at night or in the wee hours of the morning from bathroom stalls, shower stalls, and under cots. CPS officials kept confiscating phones when they found them, and told the people to turn in their phones or risk being searched, so Ammon hid his. The state troopers wouldn't allow any of the mothers to contact an attorney, either. One mother did leave the building to meet with an attorney, and when she came back, her children had been taken somewhere else and she was not allowed to see them.

My siblings reported that the children in custody were suffering in those cramped quarters. Many had fallen ill because it was so cold, and others became sick from eating processed food they were unaccustomed to. A case of chicken pox made the rounds in one location too. There was no way to wash clothing, and few people had had time to get extra when they were taken from the land of refuge, so people were forced to wear the same soiled clothing day after day.

Two of Father's older wives had been off the land when the raid happened. When they went to where their children were being held, they were not allowed to see or speak to them.

On April 9, six days after the raid, Ammon phoned me again.

"They've gathered up a lot of buses outside the shelter. We don't know what they are doing. If they don't find this phone, I'll call you later and let you know what's going on."

I didn't hear anything further for five days. Since we had no television or radio, news reports going out to the rest of the world were unknown to us. Finally, my brother Levi called to tell me what the buses had been for. The authorities had told the women with children six and older that they and their children were going to be moved to another shelter. When they got to the new location, the mothers were told to go in one door and the children in another. The mothers were ushered into a room filled with waiting police officers, who informed them that their children were now in state custody. I called Mother Annette, but she was too upset to speak; she just sobbed into the phone. (She had been taking care of Mother's children as well as her own.)

A couple of weeks later, my sister Teresa got her hands on a phone, and she described to me what that day had been like for the children. When they learned they would not be reunited with their mothers, they were inconsolable, crying themselves to sleep and crying themselves back awake. It went like that for days.

Some of them were so psychologically scarred by the experience, they would never fully recover.

And it only got worse. Officials had let children under six stay with their mothers at first, but then that changed too. Angela called shortly after it happened to describe rangers, police, and SWAT teams tearing the screaming children from their mothers' arms. My sister Sandra was nursing her one-year-old baby, hoping that would stop the men from taking her daughter, but they took the baby off her breast and made Sandra leave the building.

At the Pavilion, where they were keeping the motherless children, the younger children were separated from the older children, again pulling the little ones from the arms of their older siblings. I couldn't begin to understand why they would be so cruel to these children, and in the name of protecting them.

I tried to console my sisters Maryanne and Sandra, but I knew nothing could give them comfort besides God and His angels. I could only imagine how I would feel in their shoes, and thanked God that I had left Texas when I did. My little brothers and sisters were out there alone and afraid, and I was far away, with no way to help them. My young children could have been there too.

Father sent a message after the raid, instructing all the mothers and children to leave the other lands of refuge—R1 in Mancos, Colorado, and R23 in Pringle, South Dakota—in case authorities there were planning similar raids. Rich moved our family to a house of hiding in Colorado, not far from where his brother David was living, so he could look after us, since Rich had to return to R23.

Before he left, Rich bought me my own phone so I could stay in touch with my siblings. Mother Annette snuck a phone to Teresa in a sock, so Teresa and Josie called me almost every night. The calls usually came through around 1:00 a.m. or later. My sisters told me what life for them was like in the shelter, how the authorities questioned them about sexual things they knew nothing about. The staff treated them all like helpless little children.

Ammon and Angela kept in touch regularly as well. The state had decided some of the adult mothers were under age, including my sister Angela, even though she was nineteen and had proven so with her birth certificate, so they kept her in a shelter with her son. Angela told me there weren't enough caretakers to look after all the babies, so many of them were left in their cribs for hours, undressed and unattended. Sometimes the babies went hungry. Angela did her best, but there were just too many of them.

My heart broke for my family. I prayed that my brothers and sisters would be safe and reunited with their mothers soon.

I blamed Father for marrying underage girls and requiring other men in the church to do so as well. I never liked how Father insisted we keep everything secret. It seemed to me that if you have to hide something, it must be wrong. Because Father had so thoroughly convinced the people to keep their lives secret, the children were forbidden to tell their own truth, and now they were paying for it. The secrecy also caused the rest of the world to be suspicious, and many stories about our people were blown up by the media, or were often utterly untrue.

By the middle of the month, the state had started placing the children in shelters all over the state. The mothers were allowed supervised visits, but the children were spread out all over Texas. It could take a whole day to drive from one child to another.

I learned later that the public initially thought the raid was a good thing, that the state was protecting these underage girls. But when the media showed images of screaming children being forcibly removed from their own mothers, hundreds of people outside the church phoned and e-mailed the governor's office to protest what they had done to us.

For once, I had something in common with the outside world. I also blamed the state of Texas. They could have arrested the guilty men and done their DNA testing without taking the children away. Instead, the children were kept in the shelters for two months. My little sisters went weeks without bathing or changing their clothes or getting their hair brushed. While the children were neglected, their mothers were begging for the privilege of taking care of them.

"Everybody's going home!" Ammon said in a phone call on June 2. The Supreme Court of the state of Texas had ordered that the children be returned to their mothers. Finally, my tears were of joy.

A few weeks later, I went to Texas to see my family. My brothers and sisters were scattered all over San Antonio with their different mothers. It was wonderful to see them all. I couldn't get enough of everyone. If there was one upside to the raid, it was that it gave us all the opportunity to communicate with our family members in a way we hadn't been allowed to for years. It also allowed mothers to reunite with children they had been separated from by Father several years earlier. For the time being, Father let them stay together, although it would be as long as two years before some families returned to the land of refuge.

What made me really angry was that, while there were definitely things wrong with the church—not least that girls were being married off younger and younger—law enforcement was punishing the wrong people. The mothers and children had no say in what happened to them; they were at the mercy of church leaders, Father in particular. Separating them only hurt them more, and increased their distrust of people from outside the church. Father was already in prison—he was the one who had perpetrated the crimes and caused the pain. The mothers and children were innocent.

But just as Father's "persecution" made the people's belief in him even stronger, so too did the raid reinforce the belief that we were the true church. Days before the raid, Father had made a prediction from the Mohave County Jail, where he was awaiting trial on the Arizona charges. "Great tests and trials and great experience is coming upon the people," Father had said.

The state of Texas only made the people believe in Father and his teachings more.

The return of the children was a happy ending, but the story wasn't over. Many families stayed away from R17 while the state continued to investigate, collecting DNA samples from parents and children, trying to establish which underage mothers had given birth to which children and who the fathers were. They got a warrant to get a sample from Father in his jail cell in Arizona. My sister Teresa, who was reunited with Mother Annette in New Braunfels, Texas, found herself in the strange position of having her picture taken by the *New York Times*. Investigators had learned that she'd been married at fifteen to Ray Jessop, so the judge granted her "additional protection," which meant she was not allowed to have contact with her husband or with Father. It was a pointless order, since Father was in prison and he'd sent Ray away months earlier.

One of the underage wives, Susanne Jessop, was ordered back into foster care after the other children were released, when the authorities learned that she had been married to Father. From prison, he arranged to have Naomi Johnson, who was my sister wife Trish's mother, to be the foster mother. As soon as Susanne turned eighteen and no longer required a guardian, she joined Father's family, who were by then living at R23 in South Dakota.

In the end, most of the children's cases were dropped. But for Father, it was the beginning of a whole new problem. In July, based on the evidence collected in the aftermath of the raid, Father was charged with sexual assault of a child.

My father was no longer merely an accomplice—the state of Texas was going after him for raping his child brides.

16

Life Goes On

We moved back to South Dakota in August 2008, four months after the raid, and life returned more or less to normal.

It seemed like I was pregnant constantly for the next few years. After Rulon, I had a girl, Lavinder, who was born in 2009. Then I had two miscarriages—the first at twelve weeks and the second at just ten weeks—and both times Rich wrote to Father to tell him what had happened. Father told Rich to take me to a professional doctor to get a D&C. Then, in June 2010, I got pregnant again, and this time it took.

Shortly thereafter, Rich came to my room one morning and asked me to shower with him. I knew he'd been with another of his wives who was trying to start out with a baby the previous night.

"Rachel, what is wrong with you?" Rich said, when he could see me hesitating.

"You can't treat me like I don't know what you were doing last night," I said. "It's not easy knowing you had intercourse with another wife and you come asking me to shower right after. How can you do that?" Even though the law of purity said it was forbidden to have any sexual contact when a woman was pregnant, Rich fudged this by doing pretty much everything but intercourse with me when I was expecting.

Rich looked taken aback. I had told myself to keep my thoughts to myself so that I wouldn't risk punishment, but I had to speak up.

"I don't do for my other wives what I do for you," Rich said. "I don't shower with the other ladies when they're pregnant. You should be grateful that I give you more of my time and love than I do them."

I swallowed my pride and decided to be grateful for the attention, even if I suspected he said similar things to some of his other wives. It was frustrating that sharing my husband still bothered me, but I couldn't help it.

The following month, we received the startling news that Father's conviction in Utah had been reversed by the Supreme Court because of a faulty jury instruction. The Supreme Court said the trial judge should have told the jury that they couldn't find Father guilty unless he *specifically* intended Elissa Wall's husband to force her to have nonconsensual sex. Elissa was willing to testify a second time if there was a new trial, but the prosecutors were undecided about trying the case again. In the meantime, Texas was gearing up to extradite Father to face charges there, and he remained in prison until the various authorities decided what to do with him.

As always, Father's legal troubles didn't stop him from sending messages to the people. In August he sent one to Rich telling him to go to R17 to receive further training. Father was still limited to communication with that land of refuge, so Rich had to go there to speak with him. Rich took me with him so I could see my family.

While Rich was off getting his training, I spent time with my brothers and sisters. It was great to see them, just as it always was, but Angela told me Father had been sending weird corrections to the people lately. Many men had been sent away from their homes and families for minor infractions, like missing a men's morning prayer, or building a structure the wrong way. Often there was no reason given at all.

I didn't see Rich all day. When he came to bed that night, he was behaving standoffish and out of sorts. I put my arm around him, hoping to comfort him over whatever was bothering him, but he quickly removed my arm.

"What's the matter?" Rich had never done that before.

"Select men have been given a revelation that we as husbands and wives can no longer have marital relationships."

"Really?" I tried to hide my dismay, but failed.

"The Lord wants us to prove worthy of greater ordinances and blessing by sacrificing our selfishness in wanting to show love to one another."

I wondered why Father was doing this to us. I suspected it was because he didn't want us to have something he couldn't have behind bars.

Going forward, Rich still invited his wives to sleep in his bed, but he was extra cautious about touching us, and there were no more showers together. He gave us good-morning hugs and good-night kisses, but nothing else. He was determined to obey the Prophet, because he didn't want to lose his place in the church, or lose his family.

This pregnancy turned out to be one of the hardest because Rich was so careful not to show me too much love. He was grateful that we were having this baby—who knew when we might be able to have another?—and he treated me kindly, but the distance was hard for me.

Rich was now the bishop at R23 in South Dakota, so he received a lot of personal messages from Father. I suspected that if Father knew Rich still shared his bed with us, he would be angry, since he believed no one could control their physical desires, just like he couldn't. I got a few messages from Father here and there, mostly telling me how to be a better wife and mother. It seemed to me he wasn't in a very good position to tell me how to be a better person, but then he never had been.

I had my little boy in March 2011. Father named him Nathaniel.

The following month the new meeting house was nearly complete—it was only missing the decks on the upper floors—so we could now have Sunday gatherings in it. The structure was designed to serve as a school as well, and we mothers were excited that our children would be able to go to a real school and have real teachers.

I always played piano in general meeting, so my sister wives looked after my children while we sang and prayed. One Sunday, after we had just finished singing and a member was saying the prayer, I heard a loud scream in the hall. One of my sister wives, Susan, came into the meeting room carrying my son Rulon, who was then three. He was very pale and limp.

"What happened?" I was terribly upset.

"Just as prayer was starting, Rulon ran out of that door at the end of the hall, where there's no deck."

He'd fallen two stories onto the concrete sidewalk.

"You picked him up? You never pick someone up when they have an accident like that! You're supposed to leave them be and call 911! What if he broke his neck?"

Susan was on the edge of tears. I knew it wasn't her fault, but right then I was so scared for my little boy that I didn't care.

Rich took Rulon in his arms and carried him out to his Ford Expedition.

"Can we take him to the hospital?" I said as I followed him out.

"Not without permission from your father."

"But Rulon can hardly move. What if something in his back is broken?"

I could tell Rich was not happy with how upset I was. I tried to sweetly put my point across that I was serious about taking Rulon in for help, but it was crazy that I had to beg him to get our son, *his* son, the medical treatment he clearly needed.

"Rachel, I will give him a blessing and he will be fine."

Back at home, Rich carried Rulon into his room and lay him on a reclining chair. Rulon had a huge bump on his forehead, and he was so weak he could hardly make a sound. Rich gave him a blessing while I held his hand.

I was angry at Susan; I was angry at the men who had not secured an upper-story door where there was no deck yet; I was angry at Rich for not letting Rulon go to the hospital. I hid my face in my arm because I didn't want my little boy to see me crying. Rich took Rulon in his arms and held him.

After a few minutes I walked out of the room and called my sister Maryanne, who was living at Father's house at R23. "Please ask Isaac to tell Rich to take Rulon to the hospital so we can make sure he's okay," I said. Uncle Isaac was the most senior person in the church after Father, but he usually wouldn't do anything without Father's say-so. Maryanne said she would ask anyway.

That night, Rulon started to scream in pain. I didn't know what to do for him because I didn't know what was causing it. Aside from the bump on his head, there were no outward signs of injury. I gave him Tylenol, but it didn't seem to help much. I was a wreck—I had a newborn, a one-year-old, and a three-year-old who couldn't walk or sleep because he was suffering so much.

"I don't think I can put up with this much longer," I said to Rich in the morning. "I really want to take him to a doctor."

"Just wait a little longer, and we'll see if he starts feeling better."

I was furious. Rich tried to console me, but I turned my back on him. "Rachel, if he isn't walking in a few days, I will take him to a doctor."

I said nothing, but my mind raged. *Yesterday, right after he fell, that was the time not just to take him to a doctor but to call an ambulance. What is wrong with you? This child needs help.* I sat on the couch next to my son and wept.

Later that day, Uncle Isaac called Rich and told him that Father wanted Rulon to go to the doctor.

"Actually, I think he's doing better," Rich said.

What?

"No! No, he isn't! We need to take him."

Finally, that afternoon, Rich took Rulon and me to the hospital, where the medical staff thought we were crazy for not calling 911 in the first place. It was impossible to explain the reason we hadn't. Rulon was diagnosed with a broken pelvis, a broken hip, and a major concussion. He didn't walk for several weeks. I was not surprised at the doctor's diagnosis, given how much pain Rulon seemed to be in.

We would have to go back to the doctor repeatedly over the next few months to make sure that the growth plate in Rulon's hip was okay. I was pleased that my son was healing, but it shouldn't have been so difficult to get him the help he needed. I could not understand how Rich's obeisance to a man in prison was more important than the well-being of his own child.

A few weeks after Rulon's accident, Father sent a revelation to the president of the United States. That was how we learned that Osama bin Laden had been killed. Father's message for President

Barack Obama said that God had shown Father that the world was wicked for celebrating the notorious terrorist's death.

We might not have known anything about the leader of al-Qaeda or what had happened on September 11, 2001, if Father had not felt it was an important enough event that the people had been allowed to watch television news that day. Our grandmother still had a television back then, although most of us were forbidden to watch anything but those few children's movies my sister Becky and I had watched when we were little girls. The prohibition against television was reinstated a day or two later when Father told the people they were being distracted by the events of the world and neglecting their own preparation for Father's deliverance and priesthood blessings.

Years later, when I saw documentaries about bin Laden, the man's ability to brainwash his people to do his bidding reminded me very much of Father.

Since Rich was now bishop, our house was the center of the action at R23. Rich had an office at home, and people were always coming and going to meetings with him. There were new buildings under construction, and the crews continued to struggle with impossible-to-meet deadlines, so there was plenty to keep Rich busy.

Father's wives did most of the storehouse work, which gave me and my sister wives more time to homeschool our children (the school we hoped for in the meeting house never opened), work in the gardens, and keep our home tidy, which was a big challenge with that many children in the house.

Since none of us were having relations with Rich, the tension that had always been there seemed to dissipate. If Rich stayed out working late, the five of us would sit around and gossip to relax

after getting all the children settled in their beds, even though
we weren't supposed to. We laughed and sang songs when we
were working together at our daily chores, too, and we didn't
talk about the fact that we were all going without physical affection, but it served as an unspoken bond among us and brought us
closer.

Thanks to Father, those happy days were about to change once
more.

17

The Noose Tightens

When the prosecutors in Utah declined to retry Father, he was immediately extradited to Texas to face charges there stemming from the evidence collected at R17 during the raid in 2008.

Father's trial began in late July 2011 in San Angelo. Father had hired and fired several attorneys before he decided to represent himself. The judge ordered that one of the attorneys stay on as stand-by counsel, but left Father to his own defense.

The prosecutor presented two felony charges. The first was for the aggravated sexual assault of one of Father's wives, who had been just twelve years old. The second charge was for the sexual assault of another wife, a fifteen-year-old. While the prosecutor described the evidence to be presented, including documents, audio and video recordings, and DNA analysis, Father remained silent at the defense table.

Father raised no objections until the next day, in fact, and when he did, he spoke for over an hour, and the gist was that he was claiming religious freedom. Later that day he read a revelation to the court while the jury was out of the room: "I, the Lord God of heaven, call upon the court to now cease this persecution against my holy way." He went on to essentially threaten that the prosecution would "be humbled by sickness and death." The judge reprimanded him and forbade him from saying anything like that in front of the jury.

One of Grandfather Rulon's wives, Rebecca Musser (she had left the church after his death because Father had insisted she marry again, and she didn't want to), testified about the role of women in the FLDS and told the court that their salvation, according to the church, came from submitting to their husbands.

But it was Father's careful record keeping of his own life that had given the state its case. The prosecution only had to read what Father had written or instructed others to write on his behalf, including descriptions of the assaults on his wives. During some of these graphic recitals, Father objected repeatedly, often invoking the Lord. There was even an hour-long audiotape of Father giving instructions to "a quorum of twelve ladies" about having group sex. Finally, a DNA expert confirmed that Father had sired a baby with his fifteen-year-old wife. Another recording proved the assault on the twelve-year-old, in which he addressed her by name.

Father didn't have much of a defense. His only witness was a member of the church who didn't do anything for Father's case. It took the jury four hours to convict him on both counts.

The penalty phase of the trial introduced a raft of new information about Father's seventy-eight wives, many of whom had been Grandfather's wives before he died—Father's own mothers, in other words—and nearly a third of them underage. The state also presented evidence of all the polygamous marriages he'd performed, families he'd broken up, men he'd sent away, and additional sexual assaults on children, including his own underage brides. (The state knew nothing about Father's relationship with me. He had kept no records of that.) Father chose not to be in the courtroom during this part, so he relinquished his defense to the stand-by attorney while he waited it out in a room across the hall with a guard.

It took the jury less than an hour on August 9, 2011, to come back with Father's sentence: life in prison.

As usual, Father took his suffering out on the people. Even as the trial was under way, he continued to regularly send revelations, and life got stricter with every single one. Father had already been a big believer that cleanliness was next to godliness, but now we were required to submit a written report to the bishop saying that we had deep-cleaned every inch of the house the way the Lord had directed us to.

The directions were very specific: start by cleaning with your right hand on the center of the ceiling in each room and work down from there. Hold the clean rags in the right hand—right hands must never touch anything dirty. When the rag became dirty, we were to take it in our left hand and wash it—left hands were for touching anything soiled.

It was the same for getting dressed. We were instructed to put on our clothes right side first—right sleeve, right sock, right shoe—before putting on the left. The order of things was very important.

Our food restrictions became tighter as well. Father forbade potatoes, milk, beans, squash, peas, oats, onions, and garlic, which made it challenging to cook a meal that tasted of anything. We were encouraged to eat mostly wheat products. Women and children were also required to drink an eight-ounce cup of water twice an hour, on the hour and half hour precisely.

Laughter was deemed "light-mindedness" and therefore a sin. Children were required to have a mother's guiding hand at all times of the day, rendering them incapable of taking care of their own most basic needs as they grew older.

The people were also told that everything they possessed, all of their money and personal items, actually now belonged to the church. Every month the people were required to take inventory of their personal possessions and turn the document in to the bishop. And once a year the people would be required to take all of their personal belongings to the church store to consecrate it to the Lord; then they were allowed to take back only what they needed to stay alive.

I could only imagine that Father's incarceration had sent him over the edge, and coming up with these rules and revelations about minutiae in our lives kept his mind occupied in his prison cell.

When Father wasn't making new rules, he was sending more and harsher corrections.

Father told Rich that he was displeased with him for not meeting a construction deadline, and he was therefore no longer bishop at South Dakota. Rich was to leave R23 and take his family to R1 in Mancos, Colorado, to live.

The day after receiving father's message, Rich seemed very depressed. I went to his room and closed the door behind me.

"Rich," I said, "everything is going to be okay. I know that Heavenly Father loves you." I gave him a hug, and he lay me down on his bed and kissed me.

"I love you so much," he said. "I'm glad you love and trust me too."

I smiled as I looked up into his blue eyes and thought, *Why does Father have to tear down everyone?* Rich suddenly realized what we were doing and quickly stood up.

It took us a week to pack the belongings of six adults and a brood that now numbered twenty-two children. We took the children over to Father's house so they could be tended by his many childless wives. The little ones loved all the attention and the cooing, and we didn't have to worry about what mischief they were getting up to while we worked at packing.

A couple of days before we left R23, one of Father's wives, Lana, told me that my sister Angela was on her way to live there in South Dakota and was expected to arrive on Saturday. Father said specifically that Rich's family had to leave by Friday, so it was clear that Father was intentionally keeping me away from my closest sisters, in case I had ever doubted it. I secretly called Angela. "Why do you finally get to move here, now that I am moving away?"

Angela was as disappointed as I was. "I was excited that I was going to see you," she said.

That Friday, after the men finished hauling our belongings out to the trailers, Rich brought a small shuttle bus to accommodate all of his wives and children. We were sad to be leaving South Dakota, as it had been our home for almost eight years.

Rich had been a kind and caring bishop, and all the people there were sad that he would be replaced. Many said as much. And the sixty or so men working under Rich's direction were devoted to him. As we drove off, one of the windows fell out of the bus, and all the men rushed to help us, happy for an excuse to spend a little more time with Rich.

We had made a lot of long, difficult road trips, traveling between lands of refuge and houses of hiding, but driving twelve hours straight with nearly two dozen children was a special challenge. At first the children were excited: "We are moving to a new house and a new place!" They lay their pillows and blankets in the coziest spot they could find, and then they got really silly and wild, talking and laughing until one of the mothers told them to be quiet and calm down. My baby Nathaniel was fussy, so I was focused on him most of the ride.

The R1 property was cool and secluded, high up a mountain. The pines were giant, the underbrush thick, and there were several ponds on the land. The garden was full and nearly ready to harvest when we arrived. There were cosmos and black-eyed Susans growing wild everywhere. The chicken pen was well secured because of frequent bear visits. There were several milking cows, a bull, and a few calves that the children were excited to feed and take care of.

We had to live in two houses because there wasn't a single house big enough for our family. The men had built a huge log home in 2004, but Father had the crew break it down in 2010 because a man he judged immoral had lived there. Father even told the workmen not to save any appliances, sewing machines, dishes, or furniture because it was all marred by that man's corruption, so every inch of the house was destroyed and hauled off the land. Grass was planted in its footprint, and that area is considered corrupted to this day.

One of our homes was up on a hill and the other one down below it, next to a creek that flowed through the property year-round. Rich had most of the family live down at the lower house because it had more bedrooms. The upper house had a larger kitchen, so we made meals and ate there. Every morning, after six o'clock prayer and reading, we would put coats on the children and walk up the steep, narrow trail to the upper house for breakfast. It was important to Rich that all the children make it to breakfast on time and eat together.

Rich became the bishop of R1 shortly after we moved there,

and he was pretty darn happy about it, mostly because he was glad that he had Father's confidence again.

Each wife had her "special" job. Susan took care of the milk and made cottage cheese, sour cream, and cream cheese; Molly did the milking and took care of the chickens; Gloria took care of the garden; and Trish prepared most of the meals. All of us mothers and all of the children helped with the dishes, house cleaning, harvesting the garden, and any other general duties. Rich put me in charge of running the storehouse as well as keeping track of every transaction to manage the financial incomings and outgoings on the land. It was also my job to teach school for the five oldest children, grades three through five. I wasn't keen to do it since I had baby Nathaniel to look after, but Rich tried to make me feel better about it. "If I was one of the children and had to choose one of the mothers to be my teacher, I would choose you," he said.

There was a small crew of men on the land, but Rich's wives were the only women there. Susan and I were always being told by the other sister wives and Rich that the men were looking at us and getting too friendly. Our jobs required us to communicate with everyone, including the men, but every time one of the men came to talk to me, Rich would summon me to a private appointment with him, where he would explain to me the error of my ways. It got to where I couldn't even talk to my brother-in-law, Danny Allred, without getting in trouble.

Rich must have written to Father that the men were texting and talking to his wives, because we suddenly got a new revelation explaining that texting was not of God and was no longer permissible. We were told that we could lose our place in our families and in the church if we sent a text message. The men also got a firm correction about getting too friendly with the women.

Just living was becoming a sin.

Father's next revelation was that cocoa and chocolate were not approved by the Lord for us to eat. Also forbidden now were corn, cabbage, and cottage cheese, because these foods would make our bodies sickly.

I got my classroom ready by September 1, the day Father required everyone in the church to start school. I tried to think up anything that could be entertaining that wasn't technically a "game." We often studied by the stream when the weather was good. Sometimes I would let the children try to catch fish in the stream with their hands, and they were actually successful a few times. Other times we would go on a four-wheeler ride, take walks, or chase cows. The sister wives weren't always supportive of my teaching of their children, but I enjoyed spending the time with the kids, and the kids appreciated it.

Father's next message was a surprise: Uncle Isaac told us that Father wanted to see my sister Becky and me. He had been sent to the prison hospital in Galveston, Texas, with pneumonia. Father had not allowed me to visit him since his arrest five years earlier. All of his adult children had seen him except me, which, to make myself feel better about the rejection, I had chalked up to his guilty conscience.

Rich drove me with baby Nathaniel to Galveston on September 5 so we could see Father the next day. Becky went separately with David and their youngest child.

I was mostly excited about the trip because I would get to see the sea for the first time ever. As we got close to the bay, a sense of excitement filled me. I wanted to shout like a child as I looked over the water but I didn't. Instead I sat there as a sense of satisfaction settled over me. I exclaimed, "Oh, it's so beautiful!"

Isaac Jeffs had gotten us a room in a hotel next to the water. We had to stop there to freshen up before going to the prison hospital. When I stepped out of the truck at the hotel and breathed in the salty air, I felt a strong sense of contentedness. "I love it here!" I said to no one in particular.

We got changed and then drove over to the hospital.

The prison hospital was a tall white building with dark windows. At the appointed time, Rich and I took an elevator to the seventh floor, where we met up with Becky and David. Rich and David were going to babysit while we went in to see Father.

Becky and I showed our IDs to the attendant, and he took us through the door leading to the inmates. It was eerie to walk through iron doors and have them shut behind us, knowing they were meant to keep dangerous people inside. It was a strange thing to realize that my father was considered dangerous enough to be locked up. Even though I had been subjected to his bad actions, a part of me still felt sad that this is where he had ended up.

Inside, two guards escorted us down a long hall and into Father's room. I didn't recognize the man in the bed—he was very thin, and his head was shaved bald. *Rachel, you will act like Father looks like you remember him, even though he doesn't*, I thought. I walked over to Father and kissed him on the cheek, then sat down on a chair at the end of his hospital bed. Becky followed suit.

Becky was very nervous and fidgety. She had been going through a lot of family struggles, and she believed that Father could read her mind. I wanted to tell Becky to calm down, that Father really couldn't see every little thing about her life.

Father asked us each how we were doing. I smiled and said, "Really well." Becky said so too. He talked to us about how to be good priesthood mothers and how to raise up children of Zion.

Becky opened his lunch container, which was sitting on the table. "So what are they feeding you?" she asked as she opened it.

"Don't touch it! You don't need to touch it," Father said. I could see it was fish with rice and broccoli.

"Okay," Becky said, covering it back up and putting her hands back in her lap. "It looks better than I thought." Father often complained that they didn't feed him very well, and I don't think he wanted us to know otherwise.

"Rachel, you are on the right path," he said. "You are doing very well, and the Lord is pleased with you."

Then he said to Becky, "You need to be at peace."

I didn't want to say anything wrong and make Father judge me unworthy of any blessings, so I mostly sat quietly and let him do the talking. After an hour, the guards told us our time was up and escorted us out.

It was 5:30 p.m. when Rich and I got back to the hotel. Rich wanted to know every detail of our visit. I gave him the overview, but I had a more pressing issue. The Gulf of Mexico was calling to me.

"I have to go get in the ocean," I said. "When will I get another chance?"

"It's going to be dark soon," Rich said. "Are you sure?"

"Very."

The beach was just across the street and down a few stairs. We didn't have swimsuits—they were forbidden—so I took off my shoes and socks and walked into the surf in my dress. Rich was holding Nathaniel back on the sidewalk.

"Come down here! The water is very warm!"

"I don't want to get my clothes wet," Rich shouted.

"Please? It's so awesome!"

Rich gave in and joined me. A storm was blowing in, so the water was quite rough, but it made for a beautiful evening. The sunset was magnificent, with lovely tones of pink and lavender spread across the sky. It was one of the best evenings I had had in a long time, there in the ocean with my husband and baby. I felt happy.

Father must have enjoyed our visit. He sent kind messages to me for a little while afterward, addressing me as "my sweet daughter Rachel" or "my loving daughter Rachel," and telling me he loved me, which he hadn't done in a long time.

One morning Rich came to me and said that he wanted to take Rulon to work with him. A few hours later he called me at the upper house. "Rachel, come to my room." When I got to the lower house, I found Rich holding Rulon, who was wailing. "Look at this," he said as he started rolling up Rulon's pant leg.

I gasped when I saw the six-inch gash that bloomed on Rulon's lower leg. "We are going to the hospital," I said. "Now."

"Don't you think we could stitch it up or something?"

"You can see the bone, Rich! If you don't want to take him to the hospital, I will go without you."

Perhaps remembering the last time he'd argued for a blessing over an injury that had left Rulon unable to walk for two weeks, Rich acquiesced. On the way, he told me that while he was helping the other men pour cement for a foundation, Rulon had started playing with the jumping jack, the heavy tool that pounds the cement, and somehow tipped it over onto his leg. The weight of the jack ripped his calf muscle clean off the bone. Rulon received forty stitches that day; the doctor had to sew up the inside as well as the outside to hold his leg together.

We were an accident-prone family, it seemed. Gloria, Molly, and I were down at the lower house with the younger children when Molly's daughter Rianna and Barbie came running in breathless. "Mother Trish died! Mother Trish died!"

Trish had taken the four oldest girls and her baby on a four-wheeler ride. I took both girls by the hand. "Calm down. You don't need to yell. Show us where she is."

We followed the girls down the mountain a little ways to the stream. Trish was lying on the ground, unconscious, and the girls were by her side, screaming and crying. Trish had been driving up a steep hill when she hit a rock. The four-wheeler had tipped over on top of them, and they'd rolled to the bottom of the hill. Trish clearly needed help, so I ran to get Rich, who was in the storehouse having men's prayer. I knocked on the door, and he gave me a look that said how dare I disturb them.

"Trish is hurt bad," I said.

Rich's face lost its stern expression and went pale as he jumped up. He and Thomas Roundy, one of the laborers at R1, followed me to where Trish was lying on the ground. Her daughter Sariah was hurt too—her knee was dislocated, and her arm was broken. The other girls seemed to be okay.

Since Rich was the bishop in Colorado, everyone looked to him for direction, but all he said was, "What should we do?" Everyone was so used to needing permission to go to a doctor that even after our multiple experiences with our children, Rich and the others were paralyzed without guidance.

"This is when we call 911," I said. I took my phone out of my pocket and dialed. No one protested.

I stayed on the phone with dispatch while they sent an ambulance and a life flight helicopter. The police arrived too, to take an accident report. Rich told them that Trish had been riding with only Sariah, because it was probably a violation of some kind to have so many children on one vehicle.

Later that night, I was talking to Barbie. "Where did you land when the four-wheeler tipped over?"

"I don't know what happened, Mother. I felt us tipping over, and then I felt like I was on a pillow. When I opened my eyes, Rianna and I were at the top of the hill, looking down at Mother Trish and the other girls at the bottom." Rianna told a similar story. I was so grateful that my daughter wasn't hurt. I believed it was a miracle.

Trish was pretty badly injured. The four-wheeler had landed right on top of her during the fall and crushed several ribs, and her wrist was badly broken. The doctors at the hospital kept her heavily sedated for two weeks so she could heal. Rich stayed with her almost constantly, coming home only to shower and change clothes.

When Father heard about the accident, he sent a revelation that God did not accept four-wheelers on his lands of refuge. This was a big blow for everyone. It was hard to get around the lands of refuge without four-wheelers, because they could go where most vehicles couldn't. We used them to herd cattle, carry building supplies to remote locations, and run errands. Truckloads of them were taken off all three lands of refuge, as well as Short Creek.

Four-wheelers had become the new sin.

Trish was finally released from the hospital after more than a month. We were all so glad to have her and Rich back home. Then Father sent a new revelation that Rich read to us at Sunday meeting. Husbands and wives could no longer hug each other; only a quick handshake was acceptable to God. Father told us that God wanted us to give up our selfish way of loving one another and that we would be taught a new way to love.

It's one thing to go without sex, but totally another thing to go without affection, period. *Father really wants us to feel how he feels*, I thought.

In my heart I did not accept this revelation, which would essentially make my husband less than a brother to me. Our children would never see that their parents loved each other. And the parents would have to erase, or at least deny, their own love for each other.

I couldn't imagine how things could get any worse, until they did.

A few short weeks after she returned, Trish received a correction from Father: she was to go to Short Creek to repent. Rich blamed me for it—I could only imagine it was because I was Father's daughter. Rich was angry about what Father had done, and taking it out on me was the closest he would get to making Father pay.

A few days after Trish left, Rich came to my room. "I want you to pack your stuff. I'm sending you to Short Creek until I get a message from your father about what to do with you. You can take your two youngest children."

I thought he was joking—he had never done anything like this to me before. I hadn't done anything to warrant this kind of punishment, but I had to obey—Rich had the authority as my husband and as bishop of R1. I believed that once I wrote to Father and explained the situation, though, he would make sure I returned to the rest of my children.

Thomas Roundy drove me and the two little ones, Lavinder and Nathaniel, to Short Creek. There he helped me get settled in a room in his father's house. I wrote to Father immediately—it was the only thing that could fix this mess, or so I thought.

It often took up to several weeks for messages from Father to travel back to the people. After the expected amount of time passed, Rich showed up at my room. Father had instructed him to move his whole family to Father's family's former home in Short Creek. The house, which had previously housed Father's many children and wives, was used by the bishop, John Wayman, but Father instructed him to clear it out for us. It was far too big for Rich's family, and I hated the thought of living among my memories of the place.

Although she was already in Short Creek, Trish was not allowed to live with us.

"Rachel, do you want your mother's room?" Rich asked.

"No!" I couldn't get the word out of my mouth fast enough.

My sister wives looked surprised. "Why wouldn't you want your mother's room?"

"Because," was all I could say.

I was happy to have all of my children with me, but I hated Short Creek as much as I ever had. I missed the openness of the lands of refuge; the children did too. Here, we were surrounded by walls and the barren desert. It felt suffocating and very boring.

Purgatory

After his conviction and sentencing, Father started sending many mothers and fathers away from their families forever. They were told to leave their children behind and never see or speak to them again.

It had been more than a decade since Father instructed the people not to have sexual relations during pregnancy, but it wasn't until the beginning of 2012 that Father said that any couple that suffered a miscarriage was guilty of the murder of unborn children, because, he said, the miscarriage was caused by sexual relations when the wife was expecting. Also, if a man confessed to using a condom during sex, he and the woman he used it with were accused of murder of unborn children and sent away forever. Any person who had surgery without Father's express consent was sent away to repent. With so many people suffering because they missed their families, he decreed that if anyone took any kind of antidepressant medication, the Lord would not accept them into the church, even though he himself had been treated for depression in prison. Women who were treated by a male doctor must go away and repent.

With sexual relations now banned, Father started to accuse the people of masturbating. In general meeting, children and adults alike were commanded to stand up and leave the room if they had touched their private areas in any way. It was amazing to me that people got up and left. Did they really think God was telling Father who was masturbating?

When a person was sent away forever, the people were informed publicly. No one, including the exiled people's families, could ever contact them or even say their names. We were to cut them out of every picture, remove their names from every family record, and forget them. If a family member, including a child, even felt sorry for a person who was sent away, she too would lose her place in their family and the church forever.

It got to the point that the people came to general meeting terrified of what they would be told they or their friends or their family had done.

Father said that it wasn't just physical possessions that belonged to the church, but the people themselves, and the church could break up families if God through his Prophet so decided. In 2012, Father started to focus on tearing his own family apart.

We'd only been back in Short Creek a few days when Father sent a new message. Rich and I were to go far away from the Creek for a couple of weeks, leaving our children behind, and repent for the disagreements that had led to Rich sending me away as well as my being angry about it. Father told us that if we so much as touched each other's hands while we were gone, we would lose our salvation and everything we had.

This angered me. I said, "Rich, I can't leave Nathaniel, he's still nursing!"

"We have to obey," Rich said. "We don't want to be found questioning the Prophet." I sat down and cried.

I let all the children stay up late that night, so I could spend every last minute with them. Barbie and Martha helped me pack my things. I was so angry with Father for making me leave my children with my sister wives, who he knew didn't treat them well. All of the children snuggled with me in bed that night, the older ones crying because they understood the pain of separation that was about to come.

Rich woke me early, around 4:00 a.m. "We better get going," he said. I was resentful in my heart, but I obeyed. I kissed all of the children good-bye, cried over my nursing baby, and got in Rich's truck, and we drove away.

Father had not specified where we were to go, so we just headed down to Hurricane, Utah, which was only thirty minutes away from Short Creek.

"I don't want you to treat me like I am not good or that you are better than me," Rich said during the ride. He was worried that I would think less of him because we had complained to Father about each other, and he was supposed to be my priesthood head, the man in charge of me.

"All I care about right now is that I had to leave the children," I said. "It hurts a lot." My breasts were swelling with milk that would go to waste.

Rich called my uncle John Wayman, the bishop at the Creek, and asked him where we should go after Hurricane. Uncle John simply said, "West," so we headed to Nevada. There, we ended up in a small town in the northwestern part of the state. We couldn't find a house to rent at first, so we lived in the truck for a few days until we finally found a home with a few inches of yard and a bedroom for each of us so there was no chance of our touching even accidentally in our sleep.

I was required to sew for the storehouse, and Rich was to make furniture. Uncle John would supply us with the money we needed to take care of our needs.

Every day was bleak and dry. Most days, we did our separate

work, I in the house and Rich in the garage. Rich was kind and did his best to make me happy, bringing me flowers and writing sweet love notes, but I couldn't be happy without my children. Sometimes we'd go for a ride to take our minds off our situation, but nothing made me feel better. I worried constantly about my children and whether they were being mistreated. I tried to convince myself that I was doing God's will, but to no avail.

Rich and I were both required to write to Father so that he could decide if we were repenting sufficiently or not. In my first letter, I told him how painful it was to leave my nursing baby, trying to get across to him that it was unkind not just to me but to Nathaniel.

Father ignored my plea.

Sometimes, when we got sick of our tedious labors, Rich would record songs and I would play the flute. Once when Rich was sitting at the computer, he said with a mischievous grin, "I'm going to write a story about you."

I grabbed his hand and said, "No!"

My husband pulled his hand away from me as though I'd burned him. With dread in my heart, I realized my mistake.

"It was an accident, I understand," Rich said. "But you better be more careful." I could tell he didn't want me to confess to Father that I had touched him, and I most definitely did not.

Two weeks turned into a month. Finally, we got a call with a message from Father: Rich was to return home, but I had to go live in a house of repentance in hiding with some of my sisters and some of Father's wives. Rich would drive me to Short Creek to meet Uncle Seth, who would take me to the house of hiding.

I could hardly speak during that drive. I believed this additional punishment was because of the letter I'd written trying to make Father feel bad about taking a nursing mother away from her baby. Rich played "priesthood music" to pass the time, which only dampened my mood. As we neared the Creek, Uncle Isaac called Rich to tell him to leave me at Triplex 7 to wait for Seth to come get me.

"Please promise me you will keep my children with you as much as possible, especially Nathaniel," I said to Rich as I got out of the truck, and he promised. I could tell he felt bad for me and wanted to hug me, but we both knew we had to do what Father said or we would lose our salvation and our family forever.

When I arrived at about 7:00 a.m., Triplex 7 was basically empty—there was furniture and a few dishes, but no food. I had no way to contact anyone and no vehicle; I didn't even have the code to the automatic gate. I was stuck there all day with nothing to eat and no one to talk to. I found out later each triplex housed just one person whom Father had sent there to repent. However, the others all had food. I could only assume that none had been provided to me either because I was only there temporarily, or because I'd been forgotten.

Late that same night, Seth came to pick me up. We drove all night in the dark, so I didn't know where we were going until we passed a sign that indicated we were in Idaho. The house of hiding was called Yang. Nine of Father's wives were there. My sister Becky was there, as well as Maryanne and Shirley, whom I hadn't seen for years.

We sisters and Father's wife Alysha claimed one room to share. Alysha had been only twelve when Father married her, so she was like another sister, since she had basically grown up with us. We pushed all the beds together at night so we could be closer.

Uncle Lyle was put in charge of us, and he came every morning and every night to conduct family classes with us. He read Grandfather Rulon's and Uncle Roy's sermons to us as well as scripture. Otherwise, we spent our days sewing for the store-house while we repented of the sins in our hearts. We would break for hourly prayer.

It was good to see my sisters again, but the pain of not knowing how my children were doing weighed heavily on my heart. Mary-anne and Becky each had their oldest sons with them to repent also, but they didn't have their other children, so they understood how I felt, which was comforting and helped me feel not quite so bad for myself.

To pass the time, and to get our minds off our difficulties, we did silly things. Becky would dress up and do skits for us; sometimes we all dressed up weird, or Becky would pretend to give Alysha a "mother's blessing." (She didn't like being called "mother.")

At night we would sit on the deck and watch the stars, or lie in bed and try to outdo one another in telling the scariest stories we could come up with. Shirley would end up screaming and jump into my bed with me, and we would all laugh our heads off.

After two weeks at Yang, Father sent a message that I could be rebaptized, which would also renew my marriage, and then I would get to go back to Short Creek to live with my children. It was hard to say good-bye to my sisters, not knowing when I would get to see or talk to them again. Becky and I secretly shared phone numbers.

Seth drove all night back to Short Creek, and I tried to sleep as much as I could. When we arrived in the morning, once again I was told to stay in a triplex until someone came to fetch me for my renewed baptism. At least this time there was food.

That evening Uncle Isaac baptized me, and Uncle John's wife Joyce took me home to my family. I was so excited to get back with my children, but it turned out I was right to have worried about them while I was gone. All of the children had come down with whooping cough while I was gone, and my son Rulon had been very ill with pneumonia. My sister wives had taken him to Hildale Health Center, where the nurses said that he should be hospitalized, but the bishop had forbidden it since the child didn't have his parents. The nurses did what they could for him.

But that night, we were together, at least. The children all rushed over to me and hugged me when I walked in the door. All, that is, except for my baby Nathaniel—six weeks earlier, I had been nursing him. Now he had forgotten who I was, and he didn't dare come near me. As he started to cry and pull away from me, I felt all my anger toward Father come rushing in. Why would he be so cruel?

That night I took all my children into my room with me. I tried to get Nathaniel to remember me, but it was days before my youngest son warmed up to me again.

I didn't know if I could ever forgive Father.

In May, shortly after I returned to live with my children, Becky called me late one night.

I hadn't spoken to Becky since I left Idaho, and I hid in my closet to take the call; I knew we'd both be in big trouble if anyone found out I was talking to her.

"Rachel, I can't handle this anymore," Becky said.

"Are you still not with your children?"

"Father had me move to a triplex by myself. I can't talk to or see anyone. I can't stop crying. I just want to kill myself."

I still couldn't understand why Father was being so mean to his own children.

"I wish there was something I could do to help, Becky. You know we'd both be punished if anyone knew we were talking. And I don't want to get sent away from my children again."

"Rachel, I think I need to go to the hospital, but they won't let me."

"Becky, you have to know that no matter what Father has said about not taking medication or going to doctors, anything is better than killing yourself. Your children need you. Don't let your loyalty to Father make you do something terrible. Go to the hospital if you need to. There has to be a way to get there."

Becky started to cry. "Okay, I'll try. I'll figure something out."

When I got off the phone with my sister, I paced my room as anger toward Father engulfed me. This man was purposely hurting the people I loved, and hurting them in a way that was more painful than if he'd throttled them with a metal rod.

At the beginning of July, Rich and I received a call from Uncle Lyle, telling us to go to the meeting house in Short Creek to receive a message from Father. My heart dropped hard. By this time, Father was sending only messages of hurt. I took my time going out to the truck.

"Come on, Rachel. We need to go," Rich said.

"It's not going to be a nice message."

"Where is your faith?"

"Father has only been sending messages of correction lately, you know that."

"That doesn't mean ours will be," Rich said. I knew he was trying to make me feel better, but one of his own mothers and two of her daughters, Merilyn and Melissa, had just come to live with us because Rich's father had been sent away forever.

When we pulled up to the meeting house, I couldn't bring myself to get out of the truck. I just sat there, staring straight ahead, dread filling my heart.

"It's okay, Rachel. Come in with me."

I walked slowly behind Rich. We were met by one of Uncle Isaac's men, who told us to wait in the hallway. Lyle was the bishop at Short Creek then, but Father sent Isaac to read important personal messages to people who were sent away. Rich was called into his office first. When he came out, he was crying, and he wouldn't look at me. Isaac came to the door and beckoned me in.

Isaac shook my hand and then sat down to read what Father had sent him. "This is a message of the Lord Jesus Christ given to Rachel Jeffs."

Isaac went on to tell me that my sister wife Trish, who was already separated from her family, was judged a murderer of an unborn child. He said she was guilty because she had moved a heavy dresser when she was expecting. I knew that she had never had a miscarriage at all, but had carried all her babies to term.

The next part of the message said that Rich and I were also to be sent away for the murder of an unborn child because, according to him, we had sex during pregnancy, and I had miscarried as a result. I had had three miscarriages during my married life, for the last two of which Father had sanctioned my seeing a doctor to get a D&C, so I'd never had any indication that he'd held me or Rich culpable.

"Isaac, Rich and I have never had sex when we were expecting a child," I said when he was finished reading the message.

"You can't tell me that, Rachel. You have to write to your father and tell him."

"Why would he say God says we had sex when God knows we didn't?"

"Write to your father and explain it to him," Isaac said.

In the meantime, Isaac told me that I had to move with my sister Becky to a house in the mountains along the Colorado-Wyoming border we called Norway. It was thirty miles from

Laramie, the nearest town. He told me that I would have to leave my children with my sister wives again. "Someone will drop off food for you once a week, but you may not see who that person is, and you may not speak to anyone."

As I walked out of the office, Rich said he needed to ask Isaac a few questions. I walked down the hall and past an open door. Trish was in the room, and I went in and hugged her. "It's so good to see you," I said. She'd been forced to live apart from us, apart from her children, for nearly half a year by then.

"You too," Trish said. We hugged long and hard. I could tell she hadn't received her message yet.

When I stepped back into the hall, Rich was standing there, waiting for me. "Trish is in there if you want to tell her good-bye," I said.

"No, no, that would be too hard on me. Let's go."

We walked out to the truck and drove away. "I knew it would be a correction," I said.

"We know we are innocent, and we can stand by that," Rich said. "All we have to do is tell your father the truth, and everything will be okay." After a few minutes, he began to cry again. He was about to tell his and Trish's children that they could never see or speak to their mother again.

That evening, after Rich told the family about Trish, he explained that he and I were going on a "repentance mission."

Trish's two oldest came to stay with me in my room that night. They were inconsolable, and I wept right along with them. My children were also crying because I was leaving them as well, and no one knew for how long.

"Could Merilyn and Melissa be the ones to take care of my children?" I asked Rich the next morning. I still wasn't comfortable with my sister wives overseeing my kids, after all they'd done in the past. Rich agreed, so I moved Nathaniel and Lavinder's beds into the girls' room. I told Barbie to help with the younger ones, and I kissed all of them good-bye. I could barely see through my tears as Rich drove me, once again, away from my children.

Our first stop was over by the triplexes to pick up Becky. The message she had received was that her husband David had given her something to drink that had caused her to lose a baby. But Becky had never had a miscarriage. "I don't understand why Father is doing this," she said.

"You are good, Becky," I said. "You haven't killed a baby. Don't worry about it."

It was a difficult journey, mostly because Becky was so broken; it was hard to see her like that. I tried to console her, but I quickly realized she needed a lot more help than I could give.

Ten hours later Rich dropped us off at the house of hiding. Becky and I would have no vehicle, so we would be entirely dependent on the mystery person who would be delivering our food. Rich would be staying at another house of hiding a few hours away, close enough if we needed anything, but Isaac had told him he had to change his phone number so none of the family could call him, including me.

"Call Isaac," Rich said. "He'll relay a message to me if necessary." Isaac's number was the only one any of the three of us could have.

The house was large, with six bedrooms. Becky and I chose to stay together in the master bedroom. We had shared a room our whole lives until we were married. We set down our bags and pushed our beds close together.

Some food had been left for us, so I made us potatoes and chicken for dinner, but neither of us felt much like eating.

"Becky, if we don't eat, we will for sure not live through this. We have to eat."

"I don't think I can," she said. "I haven't been able to eat for months."

I forced my food down while Becky nibbbled at hers.

The next morning, we set up our sewing machines. We were told that we would continue to sew for the storehouse, as always. I knew staying busy was important for me, so I got down to work cutting fabric right away. Becky tried to work, but it was hard for her.

I made all of our meals, as Becky wasn't up to it because of her depression. I insisted we go on at least one long walk a day to kill the time. Once we got to the top of the hill above our house and saw a mountain lion a few yards away. It spooked us, and we ran back down to the house as fast as we could. It might have felt like a fun adventure under other circumstances.

During our first few weeks, the air was very smoky from nearby forest fires. Sometimes we could see the flames in the distance. One day the smoke was so thick, I was sure we'd have to leave the house, but we'd have to do so on foot, which didn't seem like a good idea. I later learned the fire had been a few short miles away from us.

Some of Becky's days were worse than others. She was right that she needed medical help, but I didn't know how to do that without getting us in trouble.

One morning when I was sewing, Becky said she was going for a walk on her own. After an hour or so, when she hadn't returned, I went looking for her. I traced all the paths we usually took, but I couldn't find her anywhere. It was several miles to a paved road, and I walked all the way out there, but there was no sign of her. I returned home and called Isaac to tell him Becky was missing.

"Should I call 911?"

"Definitely not," Isaac said. "I'll figure something out."

I waited and waited all day and into the night. Around nine o'clock, as it was getting dark, Becky walked into the house.

"Where were you?" I said with as much relief as anger.

"I decided to walk to Laramie to mail a letter to Father."

"But that's so far away! It would take days for you to walk there and back!"

"I wanted to give you a break from me," Becky said. "I know it's hard for you to see me like this."

"Becky, don't leave like that. It only makes me worry about you."

Becky told me a trucker named Butch had picked her up on the highway. Apparently he had scolded her for walking along the highway by herself. "It's a dangerous world out here, and you could have been hurt or disappeared and no one would have known," he had told her. He drove her to the post office, mailed her letter for her, and took her back home. I was so grateful to this stranger for looking after her, and I wished I could have told him so.

Another day when Becky was particularly down, I said, "Let's go for a walk." I was done with her believing she was a bad mother simply because Father kept telling her so. Her boys were rowdy and energetic and liked to have fun, and that wasn't allowed anymore, though it was perfectly normal. The two of us went up the hill and sat on a large rock overlooking the house.

"Becky, there are some things about Father that, if you knew, you wouldn't think you were so bad."

"Like what?"

I didn't answer, but I wanted to. We walked back down to the house and sat on the couch in the front room.

"Father did some bad things to me," I said. But then I began to cry. I had never told a soul other than Rich just that little bit the one time. The weight of those few words coming out of my mouth created a huge wave of sadness and anger flowing through me.

"What are you saying? What did he do?"

I took a few deep breaths, and tried to get hold of myself.

"You know how Father always had me with him?"

"Yes." Where Becky had been drifty and melancholy before, she was at full attention now.

"There was a reason for that. He was always touching me in a bad way and making me touch him too."

"Rachel, I would have apostatized a long time ago if I were you! You have to tell Isaac! That is not okay." She asked for details, and I gave them to her. I had never spoken those words out loud before, as Rich hadn't wanted to know any details.

It was striking to see Becky so angry at Father all of a sudden, when she had been so defeated by him moments earlier. She dialed Isaac's number on her phone and handed it to me. He answered right away.

"What's up, Rachel? What do you need?"

"Nothing really." I didn't know how I was going to say this. "I guess I'm just struggling toward Father for punishing us when he did wrong things to me when I was young."

"Like what? Tell me what he did."

I hesitated for a moment.

"Sexual things," I said quietly.

I didn't dare tell him more than that. This was new territory, and I had no idea what the consequences would be, given what had already been inflicted on me.

"Your father is the Prophet, Rachel," Isaac said. "God wouldn't let him be the Prophet if he was guilty of anything."

I don't know what I expected him to say. What could he say?

But merely saying the words out loud made me feel Father's wrongs against me so much more concretely.

For so many years, I had tried to bury the truth of Father's actions, denying what he really was. Now that I had spoken of his sins, I wondered why the hell I was allowing him to punish me. I hadn't done anything wrong. He was just trying to remind me—to remind all of us—that he was still in charge.

"If you tell Father I told you, one or both of us will get in trouble."

I think Isaac felt bad for me, because the next day he sent Rich to check on us. My husband stayed for only a few minutes, but his visit did comfort me.

The next day, it rained. Rainy days always made me feel better. Becky and I took down our hair, took off our shoes and socks, and ran outside. The cool drops felt so good on my face and feet—it felt like the rain was washing off a thick layer of stress and emotion. All I wanted was to feel the cold wetness, watch the lightning, and listen to the deep roar of the thunder as it cracked through the mountains. Becky and I ran up and down the dirt road, laughing, like we had when we were kids.

"Father really needs a hard spanking for what he did to you," Becky shouted through the raindrops.

Becky always had something to funny to say, even when her mood was dark.

We wrote to Father every week, setting the letters on the porch for the person who brought our food to pick up and mail for us. Writing the "right" letter was the key to getting our children back, because Father always said in our messages that he would know from the letters we sent to him if we had repented sufficiently.

Becky had been too honest in her letters, describing how she was struggling, which was why Father had kept her away from her children all this time. I tried to explain to her that she didn't need to confess her every temptation or thought.

"It seems like Heavenly Father wants us to be honest," Becky said.

"But you don't understand how Father really is," I said, trying to be careful not to say outright that our father was not really the Prophet. I knew that God didn't really tell him anything. If Father ever found out what we were really doing, it was only because we or someone else told him.

Three weeks in, I was getting desperate to get back to my children. I needed to know how they were doing. Then I remembered how much Father liked poems of inspiration and devotion, so I wrote this for him:

> *Holy Father, in my weakness*
> *Will You strengthen me with meekness?*
> *Will You continue Your word to send,*
> *Through Your Servant and humble friend?*
> *My heart is open to learn from You,*
> *Holy whisperings of eternal views,*
> *Your still small voice to work within,*
> *And purge out all weakness and sin.*
> *I of myself am among the least,*
> *Yet You have promised as we reach*
> *You will be there to receive*
> *All of those who truly seek.*
> *And live in sweet obedience,*
> *To Your pure word of love and peace.*
> *This school of patience that we may reach*
> *Happiness with You, on an eternal seat.*

Father, You have been a kind Teacher,
Blessings given generously unmeasured,
And sacrificing Your pure life for us,
That we might be eternally blest.
Only will You continue to ever send
That peaceful light burning within,
That someday I might with You earn
A place with You to eternally learn.

A week after I sent my poem to Father, he sent a message that Becky and I should return to Short Creek and stay at the triplexes for two weeks with some of our other sisters. After two weeks, I could be rebaptized (again) and return to my children. Becky was to stay at the triplexes until further notice.

Rich came to pick us up for the ride back home. He was very happy that I was to be reunited with our children soon, but very down that he had to remain far away to continue his "repentance." Becky, too, was doing poorly on the drive to the Creek. I held her hand and talked to her, trying to lift her spirits, but it was no use. She had been away from her children for a long, long time, and there was no telling when she'd be able to go home.

It was dark when we got to the triplexes. Isaac had told Rich to have us move into Triplex 8. "Good-bye, I love you. I can't wait for you to come back," I said to Rich.

"I wish I could give you a hug," Rich said. "Give my children a hug for me. And make Trish's children feel loved." We both wept as he drove away.

The next day our sisters Maryanne, Angela, and Teresa joined us. They had already suffered when Father had sent their husband, Ray Jessop, away. Now Father was saying that they had all slept with Ray after he had lost his blessings. It didn't make any sense, but they were told to confess that they had done what they had not.

I told Teresa to share my bed. She was so young when she'd gotten married and hardly knew what to think of everything Father was accusing her of.

We had been told to stay inside our house, but all of us girls decided to go outside and take a walk around inside the gated area of the triplexes. Shauna Jessop, one of Father's wives, poked her head out of Triplex 12. "What are you girls doing?"

"Come be with us!" I said.

"I'll have to sneak over the back way so no one sees and tells on me."

We were glad for the extra company. Shauna told us that she had been living alone for months. Father had accused her of having had sex before she married him—it wasn't true, but he refused to believe her.

That night, Teresa, Angela, Becky, and I played our violins while Shauna accompanied us on her flute. We played Pachelbel's Canon in D, which should have been totally unacceptable because it was a gentile piece of music. Maryanne took photos and video of us playing. Then we got the freezer-burned ice cream out and climbed onto the roof to eat it while we laughed and talked. We were completely disobeying the rules, and we didn't care. The security men had flashlights on us, trying to make us get off the roof, but we ignored them. We were all missing our children and our men. Sometimes you have to do crazy things to stay sane, I thought.

Becky continued to struggle emotionally, and we all tried to help her, but none of us dared try to get her medical attention, for fear of having to stay away from our own children even longer.

On August 5, 2012, I was baptized one more time. I had already been baptized three times before this.

"Your Father said that your marriage is in place, so you are married," Uncle Isaac said. Whenever we became nonmembers we were told that we had lost all of our priesthood blessings, including our marriages, but by Father's say-so we could be rebaptized and all of our priesthood blessings were supposedly restored if Father said they were. I was confused—how could my sister wives and I be married to Rich, if *his* marriage was not in place yet because he was still repenting? Who were we married to? Father was making less and less sense.

But I was happy to be with my children again after six weeks. The family was disappointed that Rich had not returned home yet, but Molly and Susan and Gloria were glad I was there to help them with the children.

Becky continued to struggle after I left her and my other sisters. She secretly called me and complained of having nothing to keep her mind occupied during the day. "Will you make a scrapbook for me?" I asked.

I snuck over to her triplex one evening and passed a pile of my letters and photographs over the fence to her, hoping it would help.

A week later I received a "special message" from Father, read to me by one of Father's closest and most special wives, Ora Steed. He said that if I told anyone about what he had done to me as a child, God would hold me accountable because everyone I told would "apostatize"—the members of the church would stop believing and leave, and I would be responsible for that.

That was how I learned that Isaac had told Father what I'd said in that phone call back in Colorado. When Father got out of prison, the message said, I would have to confess to him everyone I'd told. For now, I could no longer be a member of the church, but I was to remain with my family until he decided what to do with me.

It seemed like my father was still trying to make me feel that what he had done to me was my fault. Why couldn't he claim his own sin?

19

Back in the Fold

"Did you know we have an uncle named Wayne?" my sister Josie said.

"I know all of our uncles," I said, "and I've never heard of an Uncle Wayne."

Gloria and I had been allowed to return to South Dakota with the children in November 2012, and most of my sisters were living there as well. (Father had sent Teresa on a "repentance mission" somewhere else.) I didn't dare spend too much time with my sisters, as Father was known to send people away for socializing these days, but whenever I dared, I would sneak over to Father's family's house to see them.

"This is a new uncle," Josie said. "Father sent a revelation that Aunt Melanie was supposed to be a boy, so now she is Uncle Wayne."

Father had outdone himself this time. When Aunt Melanie was born, the doctors weren't entirely certain what gender she was, but ultimately came to the conclusion that she was a girl. Now, in her late forties, she had to deal with Father saying he'd been told by God that the medical professionals had been wrong. I don't think Grandmother Merilyn—Aunt Melanie/Uncle Wayne's mother—was too impressed.

"It's strange to see a man with a woman's hips and stuff," Josie said.

"That must have been so hard on her. Him."

This was going to take some getting used to.

It was fortuitous that I was reunited with my sisters in South Dakota, although we had arrived there for different reasons. My sisters told me they had been sent there from Texas to repent for pulling out some ugly irises from Father's garden, which upset Father's special wives, who had reported it to him.

I, on the other hand, had returned to R23 because my punishment was finally over. On September 5, 2012, John Wayman, the bishop at Short Creek, had called me to say that Rich was on his way home from his house of hiding in Colorado. It had been three months since he had driven Becky and me home.

I had gathered all twenty-two of Rich's children on the deck overlooking the driveway, and we sat in silence, waiting for him. When he pulled up and opened the door of the truck, I turned on the piece of music I had queued up and the children began to sing a "welcome home, Father" song. They didn't get all the way through it because we all started to cry. The children all ran to their father, and he gathered them up in his arms.

Rich's wives were still not allowed to hug him, but when I shook his hand, I squeezed it extra tight.

"This handshake holds a lot more than a handshake," I said.

Rich smiled the warmest smile at me.

"Same here," he said.

A month or so later, Father reinstated Rich as bishop in South Dakota, having determined that he had repented sufficiently, but his family had to stay in Short Creek. Father sent me a personal message telling me that I was not allowed to join Rich because I had spoken of Father's relationship with me, and therefore I would have to continue my repentance as a nonmember.

The member/nonmember issue had become a big deal. The worthy people were members. They were permitted to be rebaptized (there was no limit on how many times), which meant they could attend meetings, go to the storehouse for supplies, and hear special trainings and revelations. The less worthy people had no church privileges and were required to support themselves. However, since I was Father's daughter, I was still allowed privileges even though I was a nonmember. My punishment was being kept away from my husband, but I could live with that as long as I had my children with me.

By now, every family in the church was split up in one way or another. Father's next revelation told the people that members could not live with or talk to nonmembers, not even a hello or wave. Nonmember parents gave their member children to other, more worthy parents to raise.

My family did not know that I was a nonmember, and I didn't tell them. Father knew I was living with them, which I wasn't supposed to be, but I couldn't change my living circumstances; only he could do that.

Then, a month later, he *did* change everything again.

That November Father sent a message to Rich, telling him to gather Gloria and me and most of his children, rebaptize us (yet again), and take us to South Dakota to live with him. Three of Rich's older girls (not mine) stayed behind with Molly and Susan because they still needed to repent. I was happy to get out of Short

Creek—it hadn't grown on me since we first moved there so many years earlier.

Father was constantly moving his family around now to different locations all over the western United States, and it fell to Rich to drive various members to these new locations. It was expensive and time-consuming, but, as always, the people felt honored to carry out Father's will.

All this movement posed a particular challenge to Rich's family, because Rich was on the road so much and often took Gloria or me with him. It was already a big job for two mothers to look after nineteen children, but those road trips meant the child tending was left to one mother. Yet while it was a daunting responsibility, it was better than having no children at all, as my sister wives back in Short Creek did.

Some of Father's corrections were for such minor infractions, it was hard not to laugh, except that the consequences for them could be dire.

My sisters had put henna in their hair when they first got to R23, which turned it a slightly red hue. Father's special wives once again told on them, so Father sent another revelation that anyone using hair dye of any kind would not be allowed in the temple to receive their eternal blessings. He also said any woman who cut her hair, even a trim, would likewise not be allowed in the temple. My sisters were required to repent until the color faded from their hair.

When my sisters told me about this latest correction, I laughed out loud. "I'm sorry I ordered the henna and left it in the storehouse to tempt you!" I said.

"We were showering three times a day, trying to strip out the color," Josie said.

The whole thing confirmed that Father didn't really get revelations from God; he just sent corrections when someone tattled.

Sometimes my sisters came to our house to see me. "It's way more fun here, Rachel," my sister Hannah said one day. "You have all of these little children and way more of a life."

"We have so many mothers. That many women living together causes problems over the tiniest things," Josie said. "Maybe if they had children to worry about, they wouldn't always be tattling on us all the time."

The girls didn't want to leave, but then Mother Annette came over. "If you girls don't go home and get busy on your house duties, someone is going to write to Father and tell on you." And so they all got up and left as quickly as they could.

One night when I was visiting my sisters at Father's house, we found ourselves swapping stories of living alone. Every one of us had experienced it, as one by one, all the girls, some as young as twelve, had been sent to live in the triplexes by themselves. Some of them had been really scared, not just of living alone but because Father repeatedly sent messages that people in the outside world hated him and his family, and they would kill us if they could.

Shirley described how she would push her dresser in front of her bedroom door with a picture frame on it at night, and then open the window slightly. If someone tried to come in the room to get her, the frame would fall and wake her, and she could jump out the window to safety.

"What if they came through the open window?"

"Oh, I didn't think about that," Shirley said, joining us as we cracked up laughing.

When Josie was on her own, she pretended the chairs at her

dining room table were people. She'd make a big meal and put plates in front of each one and say, "Eat up!" When she found out that our sister Barbie (Father's wife Monica Jessop's daughter) was staying two houses down from her, she would send paper airplanes with notes written on them into Barbie's yard. It took quite a few airplanes before Barbie dared to look at them. She said she was too scared to because she believed she was the only one of Father's family that had been punished like that.

Barbie was twelve years old at the time.

It was a comfort to laugh at the stupid things we did when we were lonely, but at the time it had been hard for each and every one of us. The very word *triplexes* gave us chills, like the memory of a bad dream or a haunted house, because Father used those buildings in Short Creek to punish his family by placing them in solitary confinement.

Even in South Dakota, some of Father's family were living alone in different apartments and houses on the land, ordered to repent in quiet solitude, forbidden to see or speak to anyone. Even some of the young children—seven years old and even younger—were required to live in a house with just one adult, who was instructed to speak to the child as little as possible. This inflicted isolation was wreaking havoc on people's mental health.

I realized how lucky I'd been—while it was true that I'd been separated from my children, at least I'd had Becky for company. I'd seen how broken she was from having been on her own for all those months. I didn't know what I would do.

And then I found out.

On February 16, 2013, it was my turn.

That day, my uncles Isaac and Nephi came to the house to read us our messages. Rich went out to their vehicle first to hear his.

When he returned, I went out and got in the backseat to hear mine.

I was told that I was "not of full truth telling order," and that God wanted me to go back to Short Creek to live alone in a triplex with only my youngest, Nathaniel. I was to confess that I did indeed have sex when I was pregnant.

"But I didn't," I said.

Once again, Isaac said, "You have to write to your father—you can't say it to us."

"Do I have to leave my other children with my sister wives? I'd rather leave them with my sisters."

"I can't make any of those decisions, you know that," Isaac said. "For now, leave them with your sister wives."

"Isaac, I don't know if I can do this again."

"Your father said you could be back in a few short weeks. Just do as he asks, and you will be blessed." I didn't believe the "few short weeks" part. Father had already proven to me that he didn't keep his word about the duration of his punishments.

I got out of the vehicle and went back inside, where I found Rich in his room, packing. He too had been told to go far away and repent, for the same reason I had been.

"I'm so sorry that it's always about me and you," I said.

"I'm the one that needs to say sorry, Rachel. I love you so, so much. I'm glad that it is you that I get to go through this experience with, because it brings us closer to each other's hearts every time. We understand each other's pain."

At that moment, I really needed a hug from him, and I knew he needed one as well, but we believed that if we gave in, we would have lost our family and each other forever. So instead, I just sat on Rich's bed and cried.

Why was Father doing this? It was as though he couldn't believe that some of us really did obey the teachings we were given, that some of us were capable of living our lives better than he had. Not long before, one of Father's special wives had confessed to some of us girls that Father had had sex with his expecting wives, the very thing he was punishing us for now, and we hadn't even done it.

I watched as Rich walked out the door the next morning. I had no clue that I would never see or speak to him again.

Part Three

20

Solitary Confinement

All of Rich's family were told to move back to Short Creek while Rich and I repented. My sisters all came to our house at R23 to help our family pack up our things. They were sad to see me go, and I was sad to leave them again. Angela and I secretly exchanged phone numbers, as we had in 2008. We had new numbers because Father was always having the men change them for us so that we couldn't contact each other.

We traveled as a family down to Short Creek, all of my sister wives and all twenty-two children. When we arrived, Mable, one of Uncle Lyle's wives, picked me and Nathaniel up and drove us over to the triplexes. Ours would be Triplex 6. It had two bedrooms and two bathrooms. There was a nice kitchen and dining area, and a small living room at the front of the house. These buildings were new, so the living conditions were pretty good. The yard was about the same size as the living room, and entirely fenced in. There was another tall fence surrounding all the triplexes, which made it feel like a prison compound, complete with security to make sure I stayed inside.

There was nothing for me to do but sew; there was nothing for Nathaniel to do at all. There were no toys, no books, no other children to play with. I played with him, but he soon got tired of our games. There was nothing to engage him in the yard, either, except grass. I was so happy to have him, but I hated that he had to be in this prison with me.

Mable would bring our food and sewing for me to do once a week, but other than that I had no contact with anyone. Father could write letters and make phone calls and receive visitors in his prison; I had none of that. I couldn't even get past the gate because there was a code to open and close it, which of course I didn't have. I could have climbed the fence, but the guards kept a close watch on the place. Sometimes Nathaniel and I would watch people pass by through the holes in the fence, just for something to do.

A couple of times in the first weeks, my sister Angela secretly called me. "Do you really believe Father is getting out of jail?" I asked her. I was really discouraged, and I wanted her to understand that all the stupid stuff Father was punishing us for was for no reason. Father's getting out of prison was supposed to be the last great test so that we could be blessed, and I knew that was never going to happen.

"We have to believe that, Rachel," Angela said, but she didn't sound convinced.

The food Mable brought was disappointing. There was never very much, and with all of the new restrictions, there was little variety. At times, it was hard to feel grateful for it.

Two months in, I didn't think I could stand it any longer. Sixty days without my children. It felt like an eternity to me; I couldn't imagine how long it felt to them. I decided I would try to call my sister wife Susan. The sister wives knew I wasn't supposed to talk to anyone, but I decided to risk it. The worst that would happen is that Susan would tell on me for calling, but she was the nicest and most sympathetic of the four, and when I called, she answered right away.

Susan was so glad to hear from me that we talked for half an hour. She told me how my children were doing, although she didn't dare put them on the phone with me for fear of getting in trouble herself. It meant a lot to me that she at least told me how they were.

A few days later, Uncle Lyle called me to say that the triplexes were being "evicted." Ever since Father's arrest, the government had been seizing the church's property in Short Creek, so I had to move to a little blue house near his. I was delighted—I wanted to burn the triplexes to the ground, and I know every member of Father's family who had directly or indirectly experienced the punishment he inflicted felt the same way.

My new home was older, but it worked, and I was glad for the change. There was an unfinished addition that was rotting away, but it had an upstairs where I could look out over the town. There was no fence when I moved in, though Uncle Lyle fixed that in a hurry—within a week there was a high, solid barrier with an iron gate. I hated it, but at least there was no code to open it. I could go out if I felt brave enough.

I called Susan to tell her where I was, and she and Gloria came by to visit me a couple of times. Then our sister wife Molly found out, and told Uncle Lyle. He was furious with all of us, so the ladies cut off communication with me after that.

Every Sunday I called Uncle Nephi to ask him if Father had sent a message for me to return to my children. He always said the same thing. "No, Rachel. I ask him about you, but he won't say anything." It was freshly devastating to hear this news every time.

Our yard was nothing but sand, so as the weeks passed with

nothing to do—I stopped receiving new sewing after a while—I started taking Nathaniel on walks in the alleyway behind our house in the evenings. Sometimes security would stop me and ask what I was doing.

"Just going for a walk," I'd say, and continue walking. I didn't care what they told Uncle Lyle.

I prayed every day that I would return to my children. We had been taught that if we prayed in faith and obeyed the Prophet, then we would be blessed. But a little voice in my head kept telling me that everything was pretty messed up. I believe Father was trying to break me down and make me think that he was innocent, that he was a better person than me. And I wasn't going to let Father do that to me.

I began to think the most wicked thing possible: I wanted to leave the church. I wanted to find my children and go. I tried to come up with a plan, but I didn't know where to go or what I would do. I knew my mother's family were outside of the church, but I didn't know where they lived or how to get in touch with them. The mere idea of leaving was so big and scary, I would only let myself think about it a little bit. Besides, it hurt to think that everyone I loved in the church, all my family, would never speak to me again. So no matter how much I thought about leaving, I always came to the same conclusion: I had to stay.

Late one night in April, my phone rang. "Rachel, I know it's really bad of me to call, but I wanted to make sure you're okay. I heard you've been alone for three months!"

"Teresa, I'm so glad to hear from you!"

I couldn't remember the last time I'd spoken to her. We talked for over an hour. She told me Angela had gotten in trouble the last time I spoke with her, which is why I hadn't heard from her since. It was brave of Teresa to take the risk of calling me.

"Angela and I are putting together a box for you. We're going to say it's your stuff anyway, so Seth will surely bring it to you."

Rich's brother, Seth Allred, was the designated delivery person for all of father's family.

"We'll try to find some things for Nathaniel to do, too," Teresa said.

Though weeks and months passed, time seemed like one long, terrible day because nothing changed. Nathaniel and I would go to bed as early as possible, usually around seven thirty at night, and then we would sleep until nine o'clock in the morning so that our days wouldn't seem so long and boring. Each day was hot, bleak, and dry.

I tried to stay as busy as possible. If there was sewing to do, I sewed. I always did some preschool work with Nathaniel. When he was napping I would record songs for my children or make scrapbooks with their pictures. Some days Nathaniel and I would go outside in our bare feet and sit in the hot sand. Nathaniel would play like his palm was the bucket of a track hoe, letting the sand fall from his hand mechanically.

Within two months the box from Teresa arrived. Nathaniel and I were overjoyed. My sisters had sent magnetic letters, and some rocks, and a few small balls for him to play with. I knew this was their scrapings, but he was glad for anything. They also included some photographs of themselves, and a song that Teresa had written for me. When I heard it, I wept intensely. The thought that someone cared about me meant more than anything else.

Around this same time, one of my father's sisters, Aunt Marsha, moved in next door with her children. I watched them move their belongings in and get settled. I knew Aunt Marsha's girls were rebellious and hated tattletales, so I was tempted to go over and say hello. However, I didn't know if they were members or nonmembers. I was a nonmember, so if they were still members, they wouldn't speak to me, or if they did, they'd get in big trouble for doing so. Actually, if anyone talked to me at all, even a nonmember, they would get in trouble because I was Father's daughter. Father's family were supposed to be in hiding, and no one was allowed to speak to us.

I decided to give it a shot.

One evening I walked out of my back gate and snuck over to Aunt Marsha's yard. Her girls invited me right in and shared their dinner with me. The meal was so good! They had a food card, which Father forbade his own family to have, so they had a lot more food and a greater variety than I did because they didn't obey all the strict eating rules. Also, they were excellent cooks.

Soon Aunt Marsha's house became my second home. Even after security reported to Uncle Lyle that was I going over there, and he got after them for talking to me, they continued to invite me over. They were as sick of all the weirdness as I was.

There was at least a benefit to having so much one-on-one time with Nathaniel—I was able to teach him all of his ABCs and numbers by the time he was twenty-seven months old. He enjoyed the learning because it was something to do, and by twenty-nine months, he was starting to read. I was so proud of him that sometimes we'd go over to Aunt Marsha's to show off his reading to her family.

On Sunday mornings, when everyone was at meeting, the roads were deserted, so Nathaniel and I would go walking through the town, trying to figure out where my children were living.

One Sunday that May, I found them.

The house was close to the community garden, surrounded by a tall metal fence covered with black privacy film, with solid padlocked iron gates. Fortunately, there were a few holes in the privacy film, so Nathaniel and I could peek through and watch my other children at play. The property was quite big, and the house was set far enough away from the fence that there was no way to call to them without being heard by the other children and their mothers. Instead, we contented ourselves with hiding in the cluster of trees just outside the fence, so no one could see us watching. Nathaniel learned quickly how important it was to be quiet on these expeditions, as though he could sense the danger of our situation.

I was very proud of my little boy.

I continued to spend time with Marsha's family that month, helping with the cooking and the cleanup. On Thursdays the family made Uncle Lyle's personal meal. (Different families took turns preparing food for him on different days of the week.) It was considered an honor, and the people who cooked for Lyle made sure he ate well. Uncle Lyle was always telling the people that he ate only one meal a day plus snacks to save money, trying to convince everyone else to eat less. But we all knew that his "one meal a day" was a feast of seven courses, or more.

Finally Uncle Lyle got tired of Aunt Marsha's girls disobeying him, so he moved them away from me. I really started to hate him then. I wanted him to go through what I was going through: never allowed to leave his home, make a phone call, write a letter, talk to someone. *Let's see how obedient you are then*, I thought.

My days went back to sewing. Sew, sew, sew. I finished at least one dress every day. I also tried to make Nathaniel happy in his boring world, but the truth was that I died every day inside, wanting my other children back. I knew I had to be strong for them; I prayed every day, but it was no use. I almost lost faith in God. I imagined Rich was suffering the same loneliness too, though I never heard from him. Because we shared a bank account, I called the bank several times and listened to his transactions and figured out that they were being made in Iowa, so I knew he must be living somewhere there. Each day as I sat looking across town I wondered what Rich's weather was like, and if he was surviving the loneliness.

I was sewing one afternoon at the beginning of June when my sister wife Susan walked into my house.

"What are you doing?" I was stunned. "I mean, I'm happy to see you, but—"

"I'm sick of everything!" Susan said. "There are way too many children for us few ladies to take care of, and the other ladies won't hardly do anything. Sorry, I just felt like running away."

"Come sit down," I said. "You have to tell me about my children. How are they?"

Susan filled me in on everything: Lavinder kept wetting her pants, and Gloria was often frustrated with her. My poor little girl—she was just three years old—was getting urinary tract infections that made her wet uncontrollably. Hearing this made me so sad; I couldn't help her.

"I come every Sunday and watch you guys through the fence," I said.

"Really? I should have Barbie come out and talk to you next Sunday. I don't dare send the younger children in case the other wives find out, though."

"Please do! I would so much appreciate it."

I hugged Susan before she left. "Please pass that hug on to all of my children for me."

Susan promised that she would.

The next Sunday, I took my usual walk over to their house. After a few minutes, Susan slipped through the gate, shutting it behind her. We talked for a few minutes, and then she said, "I'll try to get Barbie out here without anyone seeing."

I watched through the hole, waiting for my oldest girl, who had just turned ten. After a few minutes, Barbie stepped out the front door. Immediately a window opened, and I heard Gloria yell, "Barbie! I know who's at the gate! Don't you dare go out there! You come in this house right now!"

Barbie froze in her tracks. She looked over at the fence where I was, then back at Gloria. I knew she was too afraid of Gloria to come over to me. She turned and went back inside.

Some of the other children were playing in the yard. Molly came running out to gather them up and usher them back in the house. I wanted to march in there and take my children away from those women. I realized that Susan had left the gate unlocked, so I took Nathaniel's hand and walked right in and up to the house. I tried the back door first, but it was locked. I went around to each door, but they were all locked, and the blinds were all shut.

One window downstairs was partway open. I lifted Nathaniel up to it and slid him through, then I climbed through after him into Susan's room. I walked out in the hall, where Molly had the children kneeling down and praying that the bad person at the gate would go away. When the children looked up and saw me, they stopped praying. "It wasn't a bad person! It's Mother Rachel!" They all ran to me and put their little arms around my legs and waist, but I think they were even happier to see their baby brother.

Molly and Gloria quickly went to their rooms. I suspected they felt pretty stupid for deceiving the children.

"Mother, I'm sorry they wouldn't let me come to you," Barbie said, with tears running down her cheeks. "I knew it wasn't a bad person out there."

I put my arm around her and walked into one of the girls' bedrooms. "I'm thinking about taking you and all my children with me back to my house."

She smiled. "Okay."

My phone rang in my pocket—Uncle Lyle. Of course, one of my sister wives had called him.

"Hello?" I said, trying to sound as though there was nothing out of the ordinary happening.

"Rachel, what are you doing?"

"Nothing," I said, sweetly.

"You call breaking and entering into a home that is not yours, trying to steal the children, *nothing*?"

It was then I knew for certain that Uncle Lyle was never going to let me take my children back.

"I am coming over there," Lyle said.

I knew that meant he'd give my children an angry lecture, and I wanted to spare them that. "Susan is going to drop me off at my house now," I told him.

Uncle Lyle was already there when we arrived back at my house. I told Susan thanks and she drove off.

"What are you thinking, disobeying your father like that?"

I hated everyone and everything then. Lyle kept yelling at me, saying terrible things about me, but all I could think about was how broken my heart was.

What had happened to my life?

After Lyle left, I lay on the couch, with Nathaniel snuggled close to me, and cried. I stayed that way all afternoon. I knew Father would hear about what I'd done, and I probably wouldn't be seeing my children for a long, long time.

It was August, and I decided I would give it two more months. If I didn't have my children by October, I was going to call the police. I would lose every friend I ever had, but I had to do it for my kids. They needed me. Every day I felt their need, and it was killing me. I knew I couldn't be without my kids much more. Giving myself a definite time to get my children back made me feel like I could last a little longer.

I started to make a plan. In the evenings, Nathaniel and I would sit on the fence, where everyone could see us, and watch people go by. I was done caring what anyone thought about me. I had been told not to be seen, but I wanted to be seen. I was told not to speak to anyone, but I wanted to speak to everyone.

And then, two weeks passed, and I got another message from Father.

21

Enough

"Do you really believe I did what he said?"

My uncles Isaac and Lyle were in the room when Uncle Nephi read Father's latest message. Isaac had always been the kindest of the three. Nephi was kind enough, but never broke Father's rules. Lyle was by far the meanest. In the message Father was still accusing Rich and me of lying to him about having sex when we were expecting a child. He also accused us of covenanting with each other to lie to him.

"It's God saying you did, and God knows everything you do," Nephi said.

"God knows I didn't do that," I said. "He wouldn't tell me I did something I didn't do."

Isaac got up and walked out.

"Rachel, you need to confess," Lyle said.

"I have nothing to confess."

"Do you not accept this message of the Lord through your father?" Nephi asked.

"What?" I could feel my patience draining from my body.

"Do you accept this message from your father?"

"I accept this message as coming from my father, yes. From Father." I knew God was not speaking to him. This charade was so stupid. My uncles told me to write a confession to Father and left.

That July day, it rained. It had been a dry summer, without a drop of rain through May and June, and I was ready for a change in the weather. Nathaniel and I took off our shoes and socks and walked down the road in the storm. He loved running through the puddles. I didn't even care about the lightning. Usually it made me nervous, because Monica Jessop, my little sister Barbie's mother, had been struck by lightning and nearly died. Today, nothing mattered. I was so sick of all the ridiculous things I was repeatedly told about myself.

Aunt Marsha's girls drove up in their pickup truck and yelled, "Come with us, Rachel!"

Nathaniel and I jumped in the back. Marsha had five girls, their ages ranging from sixteen to twenty-six. They were all in there. Lenore, who was the wildest and the most fun, was driving.

The rain was coming down so heavy the roads had turned to rivers, but Lenore tore through them with abandon. We all got soaked as the water splashed up all around us. It felt so good to cool off, I wanted the rain to never stop. In the distance, the sky began to clear. Then I saw a rainbow at the south end of the valley.

"Let's go find the end of it!" I said.

Lenore goosed the engine, and we took off. Of course the rainbow was always ahead of us, but we laughed and laughed, chasing it until it was gone.

I got to know more and more of the teenagers in Short Creek through Marsha's girls; they picked me up at least once a week to do something with them. One day we were taking a walk through town in another downpour, and I said, "Let's walk down by where my children live," We headed off toward the community garden. As we got closer, I saw my sister wife Molly sitting under a colorful beach umbrella while all the children, including mine, were running around in the rain. Molly looked up and saw us. You'd think she'd seen a ghost. She grabbed the umbrella and started running.

"Get in the house now!" Molly screamed at the children. "Go now!"

The children looked around to see what the danger was as Molly started shoving them through the gate into the yard.

I smiled and waved as the last head disappeared.

Marsha's girls were furious on my behalf.

"Who the hell does she think she is, treating you like you're some criminal!"

"She sure looked ridiculous, running like a maniac with that huge rainbow umbrella," I said. With that, a couple of the girls climbed the fence just to annoy Molly. We were all laughing.

This is how it was between members and nonmembers, even if they were in the same family. Members treated us like we had some terrible contagious disease. This is what my Father had wrought. I realized Father was causing a lot of people to turn into lunatics.

I was never going to make it to October. In late August 2013, I wrote to Father. I had been six months without my four older children, and I was pretty close to done. I was seriously thinking about what it would take to live alone in the outside world. It was a scary thought, but I couldn't go on like this. My children needed me.

"Father, if I say what you want me to and confess that Rich and I covenanted to lie about our relationship, I will be lying, and

God knows that. If I say we had sex when I was pregnant, I will be lying, and God knows that. I cannot lie. I believe God will stand by me if I stand by the truth."

There were days I wanted to stand on the roof and shout to everyone I saw passing by that this was all a lie, that Father was taking everyone down into a deep, dark pit. But they were all so thoroughly indoctrinated, they continued to believe that God's Prophet was incapable of wrongdoing. No one was going to convince them otherwise, especially not me.

I continued sewing diligently so that I could continue receiving my share of (lousy) food, but that was my only act of obedience. I walked whenever and wherever I wanted, unless Marsha's girls picked me up for a ride. I didn't care what security thought of me or what they reported to my uncles.

And then came a miracle.

On August 27, 2013, Uncle Lyle called me. "Rachel, your father wants your children to come live with you."

"Seriously?"

"Yes. You are still not a member, and he doesn't want you to be a member," Lyle said, "but your children are to come live with you."

I sat down on the floor in the hall, the phone still at my ear.

"I'm going to move you to a bigger house, and then we'll bring the children to you. It'll take about a week."

I was sobbing. "Really? A week?"

"Yes, Rachel," Lyle said, and hung up.

Why now? Why was Father suddenly giving me my children now?

I could only imagine that Father was starting to understand that he didn't have power over me anymore. I was no longer going to put up with this craziness. *Father better be nice to me*, I thought, *or I might leave and tell his secret.*

Whatever Father was thinking, I didn't really care. I was so glad to be getting my children back, and relieved that I didn't have to live with my sister wives. It would be just me and my kids in our own house. It didn't matter that we weren't members, as long as we were together.

On the evening of September 5, 2013, my daughter Martha's ninth birthday, Uncle Lyle's son Dolton brought my children to me. It was the most grateful I had felt in all my life. We had been apart for seven long months. When they came inside, I fell to my knees and hugged and kissed them all as tears filled my eyes. Three-year-old Lavinder cuddled up to me and cried. We all went into my room and climbed onto my bed. We stayed there talking until it grew completely dark.

"You can all sleep here," I said. It was crowded with all six of us, but I didn't want to let any of them out of my sight or my reach. As we lay in the dark, Lavinder said, "Mother, what bad thing did I do so that the Prophet took me away from you?"

"It wasn't you," I said. "You've never done anything bad, ever. And I promise you with all my heart that I will never let them take you away from me again, no matter what anyone says."

Lavinder put her arm around my neck and snuggled in closer. "Okay," she said, and fell asleep.

The next days and weeks were a time of healing, but it wasn't easy. We had all been hurt deeply by what we'd experienced the last seven months. Barbie and Martha told me about their troubling experiences with their other mothers. When Lavinder wet her pants, Gloria wouldn't let her change to teach her a lesson, leaving Lavinder to cry in her bed all night because the wet pants made her sore. Martha had spent most of her days in bed as punishment. She was an adventurous girl, and she got in trouble for anything fun she thought up to do. Rulon, who was now five, had been bullied a lot by the other children.

Now we were together in a nice house. There were three bedrooms upstairs, one for me, one for the girls, and another for the boys. Downstairs there was a good-size living room with a vaulted ceiling and lots of windows. The kitchen cabinets and banisters were all made from cherrywood.

I spent most days homeschooling them and giving them piano and violin lessons. I was so grateful for the opportunity to do the daily household chores now—make meals, wash laundry, and clean house for my children.

We were still forbidden to speak to anyone or go anywhere, but sometimes we'd sneak out and go for a hike up the mountain, or I'd ask Marsha's girls to come get us and take us on a ride to the park or just around town. Security would sometimes stop us to remind me, "Your Father doesn't want you out walking," and Lyle would call me and tell me himself.

I didn't care.

Two weeks after I was reunited with my children, Father sent a message that my children and I were to be rebaptized (yet again), which would make us members of the United Order again. Once this would have made me happy, but now it was hard to come to terms with becoming a member again after all that had been done to me and my family in the name of the church.

Uncle Lyle sent one of his daughters to tend my younger children while Barbie, Martha, and I were rebaptized. I'd lost count of how many times I'd been through this ritual. Uncles Isaac, Nephi, and Lyle were all there to perform the ceremony. There was a large baptismal font in the center of the room. Nephi baptized each of us in turn, then Isaac and Nephi lay their hands on our heads to bless us. Lyle stood by and took notes.

After that, we started attending general meetings again. My girls hated meeting and tried to find any reason at all not to go. I hated having them go, too—it was all so depressing. We had to sit in a small side room since we were part of Father's family and supposed to be in hiding. Father's family was always treated as "better" or "above" the other members of the church, so we were not supposed to be seen by anyone. The meetings were longer and worse than ever. Father's revelations were more and more extreme. Everyone had to covenant by the end of the year that they would think only pure thoughts. If you broke that covenant— say, a boy thinking romantically about a girl or a wife wanting to have sex with her own husband—you had to confess, repent for a time, then be rebaptized. The children were told that if they even *thought* a complaint about a chore given to them by their parents or priesthood head—which was any man put in charge of them—they too would have to confess and repent. Increasingly, I wondered how the people could put up with it.

In March 2014, my sister Shirley, who was two years younger than me, moved in with us for a month. Father had sent her to Short Creek to repent. I was happy to see her and have another adult to talk to.

Shirley had been married to my husband's brother Seth, but she never had any children. From the day of her wedding, she had never let her husband touch her. While she lived with us, she kept herself locked in her room because she was afraid of my little boys, a two- and five-year-old. If they came near her door, she yelled at them to get away. Nathaniel and Rulon became afraid of her because she was so mean to them for no apparent reason.

In my heart, I had my suspicions. One night she and I were talking, and I said, "It's really hard on my boys when you treat them like that."

"I don't know what's wrong with me. They frighten me."

I knew she'd never tell me the truth, but I asked anyway. "Were you abused by a man when you were younger?"

"No!" Shirley said quickly. Too quickly, I thought. Then she changed the subject.

When the boys were in bed at night, she could be a lot of fun, but having Shirley living with us was like having three more children to look after. She was terrified of mice, so of course they found their way into her bedroom. She would come get me at midnight to help her get rid of one. I was no fan of mice either, so inevitably she and I would stand on the bed or the counter while brave Martha got the mouse out from under the bed.

When Father sent her back to her husband, I was a little relieved. I felt terrible for her, but it was the best thing for my sons.

The first Sunday in May, Martha stayed at Uncle Lyle's house to tend the younger children while Barbie and I went to meeting. When we got back, Martha was crying hard.

"We saw Father," she said between sobs. They had been walking on the back lawn when they saw Rich running down the porch stairs. Unbeknownst to us, Rich was living at Lyle's house. He stopped at the bottom when he saw his children.

"We yelled 'Father!' but he just stood there and looked at us,"

Martha said. "Then he turned and ran the other way down the path." This made her cry all the harder. "He didn't say anything! I felt so wicked just for seeing him."

I pulled Martha close to me and wrapped her in my arms. "You did nothing wrong," I told her. I couldn't believe that Rich did not go to his children and hug them, not even his baby. I knew he was loyal to Father, and that Father had told him he couldn't have contact with his own family, but run away from his own children in front of them? It seemed really rude and crazy to me.

22

Flirting with Damnation

"Rulon fell out of the kitchen window!" Martha screamed from the kitchen. I ran up from the laundry room where I was folding clothes. "He was sitting on the windowsill leaning against the screen, and it gave out," she said.

I looked out, and he was on the ground, unconscious. I ran outside to him. "Rulon!"

He opened his eyes when I said his name, sat up, and put his hand to the side of his head. Then he began to cry. I was about to call 911, but then I remembered that in Short Creek, everybody was in the church, including the paramedics. No one was going to take us to the hospital without Uncle Lyle's say-so.

I called Lyle and told him what happened. He told me to wait. "Watch him and see how he does."

Tempted as I was to go around him and call for help anyway, I knew no one would disobey Lyle.

Rulon vomited several times during the night, and his head and eye swelled badly. The next morning, a Sunday, I was required to go to Lyle's house for Sunday school. One of Lyle's wives always came to pick me and my children up and take me over there. The younger children would stay at the house while the older two and I went to meeting. Now that I was a member again, we were not allowed to miss any meetings. If we had to tend children, then we were required to go the following day and listen to a recording of the meeting. Sometimes meetings ran as long as eight hours or more.

After Sunday school that day, I took Rulon to see Lyle, who was clearly alarmed by the extent of the swelling. He started questioning me like he was with Child Protective Services, trying to pin the blame for Rulon's accident on me. He asked me what happened over and over to see if my story would change.

"I told you what happened. He fell out a window."

Lyle told me that I needed to get my kids, and me, on Medicaid and food stamps before I could seek medical attention for my son. Father had previously not wanted his family to take government assistance.

"But how long does that take? He needs help now!"

I could see there was no changing his mind, so I called Isaac, since he was superior in the church hierarchy to Lyle.

"Tell Lyle that I want you to take Rulon to the hospital," Isaac said.

It didn't work. Lyle still wouldn't let us go.

It took many days for Rulon's swelling to go down. I was certain he had fractured his skull, but we never got to find out for sure.

Uncle Lyle had one of his wives figure out how to get me and my children on food stamps and Medicaid. Another wife told me that when my food card came, I was supposed to give it to Uncle Lyle if I wanted to be taken care of by the church. I wasn't happy about that; I wanted my food card. So often my kids and I had gone without the food we needed because we were limited to what was brought to us by Lyle's family once a week. If we ran out of anything before the next delivery, there was nothing we could do about it. Once, we had only a bag of rice to eat.

I didn't know then that the government had seized the church's money after Father's arrest. I can't say if that's why food was so scarce. I did know that there was a time when Father sent a message from prison that he wanted copies of his "Revelation Book" to be printed on top-quality paper and bound with the best materials. These books were sent to leaders and law enforcement officials all over the world at a cost of $2 million, which drained the church's funds, and for a time women and children in the church went without food and new clothing to pay for this publication.

The church's leaders did not have to do without, though. Every Sunday we were at Lyle's house, and we saw that his family ate much better not only than us but than all the people. There was always sugar and nuts and other nice things to eat that we never had.

When my food and mail were next delivered, Lyle's wife stood there, waiting for me to hand over the food card.

My sister Becky showed up at my house one day in May.

"How did you find me?" I was so happy to see her.

"I knew you were here somewhere, so I've just been walking around trying to figure it out." It turned out that her house wasn't that far from mine.

Becky had her two older children with her now, but she hadn't seen her youngest two in two years, so she was still suffering. She had disobeyed Father and Uncle Lyle several times and gone to the hospital for help. "At my lowest times, I remember that you said anything is better than killing myself."

Becky told me that she'd hitched a ride out to Centennial,

where our grandparents lived. She didn't know their address, but she tried to explain to me where the house was. I was really happy that she'd found our mothers' parents.

Naturally, security told Lyle that Becky had come over, and he called me to say I mustn't let her do that, but she continued to sneak over as often as she dared. And every night after I put the younger children to bed, my two older girls and I climbed out on the roof of our house, while Becky did the same at hers. We would wave at each other and watch the sunset together. It made life a tiny bit better.

A month later, in June, I was sitting in the van at Uncle Lyle's house, waiting to go to meeting, when I saw my sister Angela walking across the driveway. I jumped out and ran over to her.

"What are you doing here?" I said.

"Ha! What do you think? Same thing as everyone else does here—repenting." Angela was now staying at Lyle's with her son, and we swapped phone numbers once again.

My house wasn't far from Lyle's, so I would walk over and Angela would open the gate for me. We tried to be careful not to be seen most of the time because we didn't want Lyle to get after us for visiting. When we couldn't see each other, we talked on the phone as much as we could.

It was such a comfort to have Angela to talk to and share living-alone experiences. At one point, she had gotten very ill with cysts, which had grown so large that she looked six months pregnant, she said. She wrote to Father, but he wouldn't let her get medical attention. Angela knew if the cysts burst, she could die, so she decided to lie to our uncles. "I told them I had appendicitis, and they let me go to the hospital." She was really lucky— one of the cysts burst on the way. The doctors were furious that she had delayed. We'd all had that experience of not being able to explain to medical people why we couldn't get help sooner.

Angela's health was still fragile after that. She took herbs and natural remedies to help keep the cysts under control, but invariably someone would find out and tell Father, and he would send a message telling her to stop taking them. "It was as though Father wanted me to die," Angela said. "Why would he do that?"

With nothing else left to her, Angela started drinking glasses of water with tablespoons of cayenne pepper mixed in. Fortunately, it worked, and the cysts shrank. She didn't dare tell anyone for fear they'd tell Father, and this one thing that was helping her would be taken away too.

Angela and Becky showed up at my house together one night around ten o'clock. We stayed up talking on the back porch until after three in the morning.

It was so great to be able to talk about the member-versus-nonmember nonsense that I had experienced. Angela had been a nonmember in South Dakota, and our own family wouldn't even wave at her. If she smiled at them, they would turn away because Father had instructed them to.

"I want to go kick them all in the pants," I said. Now Angela and I were both members and Becky wasn't, and we didn't care—we were not going to let that get between us. I vowed that I would never treat another person badly, no matter what the situation. It seemed unchristian.

Angela and I also asked Becky questions about our grandparents and their family in Centennial. I could tell by the questions Angela was asking that she was thinking about leaving the church too. None of us dared say it out loud to the others, or we would seal our damnation and live in misery forever.

23

Sister Secret

Angela, Becky, and I continued to secretly visit one another for several weeks. Then Angela showed up one night in early July 2014 and told me that Father was sending her away to live alone again in South Dakota.

"Whatever you do, please keep your phone," I said. "We can't lose contact again. I think we might really need each other soon."

I would miss her terribly after having spent so much time with her recently, but it helped knowing I could reach her in an emergency. We didn't dare call otherwise, since that summer we were receiving weekly messages from Father saying that God didn't want anyone in his family to write, call, or talk to one another. We were told it was for Father's safety.

Other restrictions were imposed without explanation. Parents were now forbidden to hug their children. We were told to stop writing personal journals, or keeping any kind of personal history with writing or pictures. (I assumed this was because Father's custom of keeping detailed records of his own activities helped convict him, and he still had federal charges pending.) Father also said that rice and mayonnaise were unacceptable before the Lord. He continued to remind us to drink water every half hour—on the hour and half hour exactly—and to kneel for prayer hourly.

A few days after Angela had to move, I received my own message: I was to move to a house of hiding in Colorado with my children and my sister Josie, whom I hadn't seen in years. I think Josie was meant as a sort of gift for me, to make me feel a part of Father's family after years of keeping me away from them.

My children and I were excited to be getting out of our fenced-in world in Short Creek. We packed up all our things the same evening we received the message. Seth Allred and our sister Shirley would be taking us to Colorado the next morning.

It took us most of the day to make the seven-hundred-mile drive. The house, a four-bedroom ranch, sat on a beautiful ten-acre property near Pikes Peak at an elevation of 11,000 feet. It was a big change from the desert.

Josie arrived a day after us. I was surprised by what a beautiful, mature young woman she had grown into. At nineteen, she was now Father's oldest unmarried daughter. She was two inches taller than me, and her hair was a stunning shade of auburn that I'd never seen before, nor have I since. The way she held herself and the way she talked reminded me so much of our mother.

"Do you want to share a room with Lavinder?" I said. (The two older girls would share another room, the boys and I, a third. The fourth, we used as a classroom.)

"Sure. But Father told all of us girls at home that we have to have our own rooms so we don't think immoral thoughts about anyone else."

"That seems kind of weird, doesn't it?" I was careful not to say too much. "I mean, I never thought improper thoughts about my sisters."

"I guess." I don't think it took Josie long to figure out that I was struggling toward Father, although I didn't dare say it outright.

On July 10, I was sitting by my boys' beds waiting for them to fall asleep when my phone rang. It was Angela. I left their bedside and went to sit on my own.

"Angela, seriously?" I said when I answered. It was extremely dangerous for her to call me now. "What are you doing?"

"I don't think I can stand living alone any longer." It was hard to make out what she was saying, she was crying so hard.

"Did something happen?" I said.

It took her a couple of minutes to compose herself enough to speak. "You know what Father did to you when you were younger?"

I sat up. I had never said anything to her about it.

"Rachel? Are you there?"

"Yes." My hands were starting to shake.

"I know you know what I'm talking about," Angela said.

"How do you know about it?"

"Because he did the same things to me."

"I had no idea," I said. "I thought I was the only one."

The tears I cried then were ones of relief.

"I am so sorry Father did that to you, but I am so glad to know that someone understands me. That someone believes me. But how did you find out he did it to me?"

Angela told me that when Becky was putting together my scrapbook at the triplexes, Angela had seen some of the letters Father had written to me, asking my forgiveness. "I knew right away what he was referring to."

Father had started abusing Angela when she was six years old, doing the same things to her he had been doing to me for two years by then. Everything she said brought back memories and images of those years. Angela told me Father laid the blame for it on her, just as he had laid it on me. "Angela, when I told you to touch me," he told her, "I was just testing you to see if you wanted to do it. You did it, so that shows me you have immoral desires." Father continued abusing her until she was ten years old.

"Why do you suppose Father has kept you and me alone so much?" Angela said. "It's because of this."

"I think so, too. Someday we are going to have to leave." I had finally said it. "Now I feel like I can, thanks to you. Because you understand."

"Same here," she said.

We kept talking the whole night long, both of us so relieved to finally be able to shine a light on our deepest, darkest secret. It was a moment of alleviation for me. Having someone else hear and accept my truth was wonderful beyond description.

24

First One Out

Josie, my kids, and I had a lot of fun together in Colorado. We prepared meals together, and Josie helped me teach school in the mornings. In the afternoons, we'd go have adventures in the woods, taking hikes and exploring. Josie and my girls hung a rope over a branch of a big tree and made a swing out of it. Sometimes we'd go looking for a "bendy" tree and bounce the kids on it.

So high up in the mountains, we saw a lot of wildlife. Hermit thrushes sang their beautiful spiraling songs that reached right into your heart every morning and every evening; mountain bluebirds shone in the thin air. The mule deer would come right up near the house; they didn't see a lot of people, so they weren't afraid of us. We found bear scratches on many of the aspens around us, and even a cougar's claw marks up a tree trunk to the very top.

Father sent a message that we weren't allowed to go walking in the woods, but Josie and I silently agreed that was ridiculous, and we continued our adventures.

Angela and I continued to talk on the phone late at night.

Father was still obsessed with my sexual relationship with Rich. He sent a message commanding me to confess that Rich had sexually abused me. I wanted to write him back, "The only person who has sexually abused me was you." I didn't dare. Instead, I told him honestly that Rich had been a very kind and loving husband and had never purposely hurt me.

Father didn't like my response. We'd been in Colorado just three weeks when he sent a message that my kids and I were non-members again, and we were to move back to Short Creek. Josie was supposed to go to South Dakota.

I couldn't figure out what Father wanted from me anymore. This never-ending stream of corrections seemed pointless, and I was getting tired of the weird messages he kept sending. (Not to mention I was really sick of moving.)

The only good thing about going back to Short Creek was that I would be near Becky once again. We had been assigned to a different house than we'd been in before Colorado, but it was still just down the road from hers. She came to visit daily, walking to my house in plain view of security. Neither of us cared about the corrections that might result.

My cousin Sherilyn was moved into a small camp trailer nearby. She had just turned sixteen and had been sent to live alone and sew. I was told to take her her meals, but we were not to speak to each other. Sixteen was too young for this punishment. I tried to get her to talk anyway, but she didn't dare.

Even though Angela was in a nicer place than I was, she was worse off because all the members in South Dakota treated her badly. Our conversations now always included some version of this exchange:

"I'm going to leave soon. I really want out."

"Just wait a little longer."

Finally, Angela decided it was time—it was August, and she was done. She had been apart from her husband since before her child was born, and her son was now eight years old. She had lived her entire life as a mother living in Father's house, and the last two she and her son had lived alone.

"Rachel, you have to help me get a phone number for our relatives in Centennial so they can come get me."

"I don't know how, but let me think about it. If the church finds out I helped you, I'll get in big trouble."

The next day, I remembered that you could call information to get a phone number. "Angela, if you dial 411, you can ask for any number you want. Tell them you're looking for Dorothy Barlow in Centennial or Tom Barlow in Cane Beds." Becky had told us our uncle's name and we had met our grandma when we were very young: Dorothy was our mothers' mother, our grandma, and Tom was their brother, our uncle.

It took Angela several tries, but she finally found Uncle Tom's number. She called him, and he agreed to come get her from South Dakota in a week's time.

"He's going to come late at night, so I can sneak out to his car without anyone seeing me," Angela told me.

As the week passed, my sister kept me updated on her plans and what she was doing. She asked me to give her the directions to R23 to share with Tom, because I had lived there longer and knew the place better than she did. During that week she got two messages of correction from Father, telling her that she was not "of full truth telling order" in her confessions and that she needed to confess more. She was scared Father would stop her.

The day of Angela's scheduled departure, Becky was over at my house and overheard me on the phone with her. In a moment of righteousness, Becky was compelled to call our Uncle Isaac and tell him that Angela was leaving that night.

"Why did you do that?" I said to Becky. I couldn't believe she would give Angela up like that.

"Well, we can't just let her go," Becky said defiantly, even though she was the one who'd gone so far as to find our grandparents on the outside.

"Yes, we can!" I said. "It's her choice, and that's what she wants to do."

Later, Becky said she felt guilty, knowing that Angela was leaving; the years of being taught that leaving was a sin made her feel like she had to report it.

Isaac called Angela immediately and told her she was committing the worst sin possible, reeling off the list of terrible punishments that would follow her into the depths of hell. Angela's mother, Mother Annette, went over to Angela's house and told her she was wicked to do this.

Angela wasn't having any of it. Done is done, and with Uncle Tom ready to help her, she stood up to them. She told Mother Annette, "Father abused me and Rachel as children." At first Mother Annette was angry at Father, and then she said, "Father has suffered for his wrongs, and the Lord has forgiven him."

Angela left with Uncle Tom that night.

Isaac called me to find out what my role in her escape was. I wasn't about to tell him anything. I cried on the phone so I wouldn't have to speak.

Four days later, Isaac called again. "You go out to Centennial where Angela is staying, and bring her back," he said. "Make her come home. She can live with you if she wants, but your father wants her back." They knew that Angela loved me and usually listened to what I said.

Uncle Lyle had someone deliver a vehicle to my house, and Becky and I drove to Grandma's house. I had asked if Becky could come to show me the way, and Uncle Isaac told me she could.

When we arrived, my grandma and some of our other relatives greeted us at the door. I had not met most of these people, but they were all very kind and welcoming and invited us in. We sat with them in the living room for about twenty minutes, while they did their best to make us comfortable. My grandma showed us photographs of our mothers' family. We had not been in a non-church house since we were very young. Everything and everyone was so different from the life we knew, it was hard to know what to say or do.

Angela took me upstairs to her bedroom. "I'm supposed to bring you back," I said, half laughing. I didn't know what I wanted for Angela. It was confusing for me, because I was still in the church, listening to all the terrible things everyone had to say about Angela. Still, I knew it was hell there.

"After everything I've been through? I will never go back to that."

I already knew that. I was happy and sad for her all at the same time. We talked for a little while, and then Becky and I returned to Short Creek without her.

A week later, one of Father's wives who'd been living with Becky brought me a letter. It was from Becky. I guessed what it said before I read it: she and her two older boys had gone to join Angela. And she wasn't about to leave her two younger sons behind, either. Clearly, the guilt she'd felt when Angela left had dissipated.

This is what had happened: Uncle Tom had called the bishop's office and told them they had two days to bring Becky's two younger children, or else he would go to the police. (Becky's boys had been living in a house of hiding in Colorado with some of Father's family.) Our uncles Lyle and Isaac had no choice but to bring the children back to Short Creek, and two days later, Robert, Rich's brother, met Becky at a park in Short Creek with the boys. Uncle Lyle had Becky's sister wife, Rosa, try to convince Becky to sign adoption papers and let her take Becky's children permanently, but Becky refused. Uncle Tom was there with Becky, giving her support and helping her to be strong against the pressure she was getting to sign over her boys. Tom helped Becky get the boys into his vehicle, and they drove away.

Uncle Lyle guessed, correctly, that I was likely to follow Angela and Becky out, so he moved me and my children into a walled-in, iron-gated property. Lyle clearly didn't want me to have any contact with or access to my sisters, but what he couldn't have guessed was that not only did I have Uncle Tom's number, but Tom had already given me Becky and Angela's new numbers too (they didn't have their church phone numbers anymore). I talked to my sisters all the time, and late at night, they would come pick me up and drive me out to their house to hang out, giving me a preview of what life could be like on the outside. We watched the movie *Titanic* together on DVD—it was the first movie I'd seen since Becky and I saw *Bambi* when we were little girls.

I was so ready to join my sisters and leave, but there was one thing holding me back: I wanted to talk to Rich. I wanted him to leave with me and the children. But I had no way to contact him, and I didn't know where he was, so I decided to wait a little longer in hopes that an opportunity would present itself.

In the meantime, I was increasingly brazen about leaving my house with my kids. Some days we'd go to the park to play basketball with some of Marsha's kids' friends, or to town. Rich's younger brother Danny sometimes gave us money so we could get some of the things we desperately needed, like food, jackets, and paper and pencils to keep the children busy. Becky had stayed in touch with our brother-in-law, and she had given me his number during our secret meetings. Danny had always been kind, and didn't mind breaking the rules to help us. Since he wasn't married, and worked for Phaze Concrete—a company owned by the church in Short Creek—he had money.

The FBI was monitoring Father's family, so when they learned that Angela had left, they sought her out. She told them that Sherilyn, my cousin, was underage and living alone. The Washington County sheriff called me to confirm Sherilyn was where Angela said she was and that she was indeed just sixteen, and I did so. The FBI rescued her and took her to her father, who had been sent away forever several years earlier. Sherilyn eventually ended up back with her mother, who was still in the church, but at least she didn't have to live alone anymore.

Angela also told the FBI that Uncle Lyle had taken my food card away, just as he had taken all the food cards from the women he was "taking care of." The agents told Angela to tell me that I could call the Utah Department of Economic Security and say my card was stolen, and they would send me a new one. I did, and had them send the card to a friend's P.O. box so that no one would know I had it, since my mail was usually given to me by whichever of Lyle's wives was in charge of bringing my food each week. It was so nice to have real food again.

Life continued for a few months. My kids and I had to move one more time when one of Uncle Lyle's daughters, Hillary, decided she wanted my house. Still, I heard no word from Rich, and I knew nothing of his whereabouts. Wasn't he even curious about his children?

Then one day, in December 2014, when my kids and I were on our way to go sledding with some of my friends at Brian Head near Cedar City, Utah, Uncle Isaac dropped the hammer:

"Rachel," Isaac said, "your father is not pleased with your socializing and leaving home. He is having you move to Lyle's place so no one can talk to you." I held the phone to my ear, stunned but silent. "Are you there, Rachel?" he asked.

"Yes," I said. "Isaac, I really don't want to live with Uncle Lyle." Uncle Lyle's house was gated and walled and guarded. Moving there would be a life sentence, worse than Father's in jail. Like him, I'd never get out.

Isaac chuckled a little and then said, "Yes, I understand, but you have to obey your father, and this is what he wants."

I tried to have fun on the mountain that day, tubing in the snow with my friends, but inside my mind churned in turmoil. Did I risk going to Lyle's in hopes of seeing Rich again? What was the point, if we were all trapped there? I realized that I had a big decision to make. The time for waiting had passed.

That night Lyle called me himself and accused me of immoral behavior because I had been leaving my house and participating in forbidden (if harmless) recreation. He reminded me that fun was a sin.

"No," I said. "I've done nothing wrong. I don't think the way you think. I'm not like you."

I could hear him gasp. Lyle was the bishop; nobody spoke to him like that.

"Rachel, I'm sending my boys over tonight to move you," he said, his voice taut with anger.

"No, Lyle, I don't want to move to your house tonight."

"You have defied your father, Rachel, and you must come live here and repent."

I wasn't going to win this argument, and frankly I was afraid of Lyle. Father had always issued his corrections in a measured tone of voice, but Lyle was a big man who screamed. The best I could do was buy some time.

"At least wait until tomorrow morning," I said. "It's going to take me hours to pack all of our things and get the children ready."

"The boys will be there first thing," he said, and hung up.

I lay on my bed with my hands on my head. My stomach felt sick at the thought that I had to leave the church now, without seeing Rich. I picked up a framed picture of Rich that was by my bed. "I'm sorry, Rich," I said to his image, "but I have to do this." Then my eyes filled with tears. I picked up my wedding scrapbook and started leafing through it. *Rachel, you're making this way harder.* I closed the book and stood up. I had work to do.

I went downstairs and locked the outside doors. Then I called Angela. "Come get my children. I have to pack."

25

Over the Wall

"A city marshal is following us," Angela said, panic in her voice. I stayed on the phone with her during the fifteen minutes or so it took Becky and her to make the drive to my house, while I packed up a few things for them to take for the night. With guards making regular passes around the house to make sure I was behaving, we had to time their arrival perfectly. I was sure Lyle would have increased surveillance after our conversation earlier, but we had the advantage of darkness to help us accomplish our mission without detection.

Now this.

"You have to lose him!" I said. The marshals were employed by the city, but the men were members of the church, so they acted as security for Uncle Lyle.

"We'll keep driving around, Rachel."

"The longer we can keep Uncle Lyle from knowing that I'm leaving, the better."

The children were playing in their rooms, oblivious to what was about to happen. I paced with the phone to my ear. "Well? Did you shake the marshal?"

"We're going to circle one more block. Hang on." I wanted to stand by the window to look for them, but I didn't dare move the curtains in case someone was watching me from the roof across the street. I couldn't see that far in the pitch-black.

After a few minutes Angela said, "Okay, I'm almost to your house. Have your children out by your gate, ready to jump in."

I ended the phone call and went to get the children. "Everybody, put your shoes on. Your aunts are coming to get you for a sleepover with your cousins. Hurry!" I didn't want to explain what was really happening until later so they wouldn't ask a lot of questions. I lined them up by the door. "Shh, it's late, so we have to be very quiet. Ready?"

I opened the door and quickly walked the children down to the gate just as Angela and Becky pulled up. I opened the rear door and whispered to the children, "Quick, get in before anyone sees."

All five piled into the backseat, I shut the car door, and Angela hit the gas. I saw little hands in the rear window waving goodbye to me before the car turned out of sight.

I ran back into my house and locked the front and back doors. I had to pack up the belongings of one adult and five children.

I set to work packing clothes and photographs and scrapbooks, my heart breaking anew every few minutes. I couldn't help but think of all the people I loved and how they would now think I was the most terrible person in the world for denying everything I had been taught to believe. Father had often said, "When a person chooses to leave the priesthood, they are severing their right to their heritage and priesthood blessings. There is no salvation for them." My family and friends still believed what he said and would certainly disown me. My sisters and brothers who stayed behind, Father's wives who had helped raise me, my own husband—they would all be in the past of my life.

Just as the sun was beginning to peek above the horizon,

around seven o'clock, there was a dreadful pounding at the front door.

"Rachel! We've come to move you to Lyle's house!"

His boys, right on schedule.

I sat on one of the children's beds, silent.

Pound! Pound!

"Rachel! We know you're in there!"

Still I said nothing. I was afraid to so much as stand for fear they would hear the floorboards creak.

Pound! Pound! Pound!

"We're not leaving, Rachel. We've got all day."

Ring! My cell phone lit up, and I pushed it away from me on the bed. I was afraid to even touch it. The phone light dimmed, the call ended. I heard the *ping* indicating a message. *Ring! Ring!* Every time the screen lit up, it felt like a rebuke.

Eventually the pounding stopped, but the men didn't leave. I snuck a peek out the window—the men were sitting on my porch.

By 8:00 a.m., I had eleven missed calls from Lyle and seven from Isaac. All I could do was wait and try to keep my cool, but I was as frightened as I'd ever been in my life.

Bang! Bang! "Rachel!"

By noon, Lyle was there banging on the door himself and bellowing my name. I flinched every time he slammed his fist against the front door. I could hear him talking in muffled tones to his boys, but I couldn't make out what they were saying. And then all was silent.

BANG! BANG!

I jumped. The sound was coming from the other side of the house. He was at the back door, pummeling it with his fists and jiggling the knob. I was afraid he was going to break right through the wooden door and come for me. I grabbed my phone, ran to my bedroom, and locked the door.

"Rachel! Do not ignore me!"

I went into my bathroom and locked that door too. I sank to the floor and wrapped my arms around my bent knees, shaking with fear.

"You are disobeying the Prophet, Rachel. Your father has ordered that you come live in my house." *BANG!* "You must obey your father!"

I could hear the windows shaking all over the house from the force of his fists against the door. I stayed on the bathroom floor until midafternoon, when the noise finally stopped.

Gingerly, I unlocked the door and tiptoed through my bedroom to the window. There was no sign of anybody there. I went to the girls' room on the other side of the house and looked out. The men had left the porch, and there was no vehicle in front.

Now I just had to wait until dark. The phone continued to ring throughout the afternoon, like some tiny monster come to life. I dared not answer Lyle's and Isaac's calls.

I was still shaking hours later when my brother Ray, Brenda Jessop's son, called. Ray had been in hiding just as I was, and we had visited several times after he discovered where I was. "Can I stop by?" He had no idea what had just happened.

"Yes, but you have to be fast." I didn't explain why.

The bags with my children's belongings and mine were upstairs, so Ray didn't see anything amiss when he came over.

"Father is sending me to live with your husband," Ray said. He told me that Rich was living with some of Father's other sons at the Norway house of hiding in Colorado, where Becky and I had stayed. It made my heart hurt to hear Rich's name. What I was about to do was going to hit him hard.

Ray and I talked for a little bit, and then he asked, "Why did Becky and Angela leave?"

My internal filters had fallen away. I told him the truth about what Father had done to me and Angela, and I watched as the blood drained from his face.

When my phone rang, and I didn't answer it, Ray said, "I should go." He knew it wasn't safe for him to be seen with me.

"Security is watching me," I said.

I retreated to my bedroom after he left. Lyle and his sons came back to see if I would let them in, but they didn't stay long that time.

That evening my friend Sharon Allred, Rich's cousin, snuck in to see me for a few hours while I waited for the cover of darkness. Sharon was in her early twenties, and I had gotten to know her through Marsha's girls. She was a nonmember forced to live away from her family in Short Creek, like so many of us. I was near bursting with what I was planning to do, so I told her I was leaving, and she was completely supportive.

We sat in my room with the door locked, eating ice cream like naughty little girls, while the phone continued to ring and I continued to ignore it.

"Wouldn't it be funny if Uncle Lyle broke open the door and came in here and saw us this way, then sent a letter to Father that said, 'I found Rachel in her room eating ice cream!'" Several of Father's revelations had said that God did not approve of ice cream anymore. We laughed until the banging on the door returned, louder and more terrifying than before.

At eight o'clock Sharon snuck out the back door, but security saw her leave my house and called Lyle, who gathered her up right away to find out what I was doing. Thankfully, she didn't tell him, as she told me in a text message.

By nine, it was fully night, and I called Angela.

"Can you come get me? I'm ready. I don't think anyone is watching right now." Lyle's guards usually worked around the clock, but I couldn't see any of them on duty just then.

I brought all the bags I'd packed downstairs, set them by the front door, and stepped outside to wait. There was a note pinned to the door. I recognized Lyle's handwriting: "Rachel, please do not leave. You can live wherever you want."

I laughed out loud. I hadn't slept in thirty-six hours, my nerves were raw from the day's constant onslaught, and now he was telling me I could call the shots if I stayed?

After what you've put me through? I don't think so.

I brought everything down to the gate to wait. I was shivering in the late-December cold. Despite the conciliatory tone of Lyle's note, the fear of being found out made me shiver harder. I didn't know when the guards would return, but I was certain they would.

Hurry, Angela! Hurry! I thought as I stood huddled by my bags. Several trucks passed by, causing me to duck for fear it was security coming to get me. It wasn't so much relief I felt when they continued without stopping as merely a pause in the sense of dread that had been with me since the previous night.

I don't know what miracle cleared the roads when my sister finally pulled up to the curb in front of my house, but there was no one around to see us as we jammed my family's belongings into the back of the car and drove away from Short Creek for the last time.

In the brief time Becky and Angela had been out, Grandma had gotten a four-bedroom apartment for my sisters and their children, so that's where they took me that night. When we got to the apartment, I hugged my kids, then went into what would be my bedroom, shut the door, and cried.

It was hitting me all at once what I had just done. I would never see Rich again. My children would never see their father again. I would never see or speak to all of my family still in the church. I would have to figure out on my own how to support five children, and fast.

But first, I got to experience my first party.

I hadn't paid attention to the calendar when I was planning my escape, so it was mere chance that the day I left was New Year's Eve. The party at Grandpa's house was wild and fun and a culture shock, for sure. Grandpa's family was very large, since they lived polygamy even though they weren't in the church. Our aunts and uncles filled the large living room, where all kinds of food and wine were served. It was my first taste of wine, and I only had a little because I wasn't used to it. (It was not my first alcohol. When Becky and I were eighteen, we did a pirate skit using unopened beer bottles as props. Alcohol wasn't technically allowed, but Father let Mother Annette keep some in the fridge when she was nursing a baby. When we finished our performance, we had asked Father if we could drink the bottles of beer. He told us, "Yes, if you drink the whole bottle all at once," and we did. Then Father had fun making us walk a straight line, which we could do because we weren't drunk, but I did have a massive headache the next morning.)

That New Year's Eve we played games and some of the aunts and uncles told crazy, funny stories that had us all grabbing our bellies laughing. I hadn't been around people who dared to laugh for such a long time that I had to keep telling myself, *It's okay to laugh now, Rachel*. At midnight the revelers, many of whom were a little drunk by then, stood to sing a joyful, slightly out-of-tune "Auld Lang Syne."

As I lay down in bed that night, I told myself, "This is going to be okay." But I had a hard time sleeping that night. My daughter Martha, ten years old then, couldn't stop crying—she believed we were making a terrible mistake and was sad that she would never see her father or her other brothers and sisters again.

"Do you want to go back?" I said. "I'm staying here, but you can go back if that's what you want."

"No! I just want to see our family again."

"Hopefully some day they will leave too, and then we can see them," I said. "We have to pray that they will. That's all we can do right now."

Eventually Martha settled down to sleep, but I tossed and turned, thinking about what I had just done to my family.

The next day all of my uncles on my mother's side of the family got a trailer ready and drove over to my house in Short Creek to gather up the rest of my belongings. I did not want to go with them because I knew that Uncle Lyle would have someone there, waiting to convince me of the error of my ways, so my sister Angela went with them.

When they drove up to my house, there was security all around. Some of the security men had cameras set up on a deck across from my house to document my apostasy.

When my uncles and sister Angela walked into my house, they saw my sister wife Gloria with three of her sisters, waiting to talk to me. Uncle Lyle had told Gloria to wait at my house until I came to get my stuff so that she could give me a message. She asked Angela, "Where is Rachel?" Angela said, "She's not here." Gloria and her sisters stood there with their arms folded, one of them taking notes of the proceedings, trying to intimidate my uncles and sister, but instead my uncles made jokes as they moved furniture and boxes, making the situation as light as possible.

When they brought my stuff, I found a letter from Gloria in the top drawer of my dresser. In it she tried to convince me that what I was doing was terrible. "Rachel," she wrote, "you are the person that brings fun to our family. We won't be happy without you."

The news of Father's girls leaving spread like wildfire, and people in the community came out of the woodwork to help us. We were really lucky to have people who loved us and cared for us.

Our relatives were not very well off, but they helped us as best they could. My brother-in-law Danny Allred bought me a used Toyota Corolla so that I had a way to get around. A friend had given Angela $500 to help her out, and she turned around and gave it to me to buy real clothes for myself and my children. My sisters were already dressing in normal clothes. For the first couple of days I wore a skirt, because that's what I was used to. Then Angela let me borrow a pair of pants, and I was hooked. I loved the freedom pants gave me. My girls quickly changed over, too—they especially loved choosing their own things, going for the brightest and most elaborately decorated shirts they could find. We were so used to plain pastels that having access to clothes with design and character was exciting for all of us.

We bought food with food stamps, for which we were grateful. We had access to whatever we wanted to eat now, which was a welcome change for all of us; squash and rice and sugar if we wanted it. I was never so happy to see onions and garlic in my life.

Within a week, I had put my children in public school for the first time. It was a huge change for them, and I had to convince them they would be okay. There were many ex-FLDS children enrolled, so at least I didn't have to have awkward conversations with the administrators about why my kids didn't have school records or why they were behind in social studies, world history, and science (Father had banned those subjects). My kids didn't know how to make friends, though, and they didn't relate to the other students, but the teachers were kind in helping the children adjust to their new life.

Angela started giving violin lessons, and already had a number of students. I started to do the same. Since everyone in that area knew who we were and that we played the violin well, we didn't have to advertise. Many people simply came asking for lessons.

I wasn't there very long before I realized that I didn't want to stay in Centennial. A lot of people there lived polygamy by choice, and I couldn't see myself living that way again. The men in town all looked at "single" women like my sisters and me as potential wives to add to their families. I wasn't interested.

Of course, Father wasn't happy with us, and he sent our uncles to track us down. They couldn't call me because I had gotten a new phone, so they started following us and showing up at our apartment late at night. One morning, as I was dropping my kids off at school, Uncle Seth Jeffs showed up and put a phone to my ear. "Here, Rachel, say hello."

I was so startled I didn't know what to do, so I said, "Hello?"

Uncle Lyle started right in reading a message from Father. "Thus saith the Lord to Rachel Jeffs . . ." The priesthood never takes children away from their mothers, Father said, so if I didn't return to the church, I would be guilty of "murder of the living order" because I had taken my children away from the church. Considering he sent mothers away from their children all the time, I didn't think it was much of an argument.

This effort to get us back was a first—everyone who had left before us was barred forever, end of story. Even Lyle remarked, "This is a great privilege, because the Lord has never allowed any other apostates to come back."

Later that day, Becky told me, Seth had followed her all over town. She sped dangerously down dirt roads and clear out to the airport just to get away from him. Several days later, Seth approached Angela and me and tried to give us another message. "Sorry, Uncle Seth," Angela said. "We cannot trust Father because of what he did when we were young." With that, we turned and walked away.

Another time Uncle Isaac, who had gotten my number from one of my friends in the church, called me. "We will buy a house for you anywhere you want if you will just live under the direction of the priesthood."

But I couldn't do that to my children again. It was amazing to me that Father was suddenly promising all of these wonderful things if we would just come back.

Becky, Angela, and I were all getting pretty tired of these men following us, so we finally told the FBI what was happening, and they offered to help us. The next time someone from the church approached us, we told them that the FBI was involved, and they started to leave us alone more.

Becky was still recovering from her breakdown. She turned to one of our mothers' brothers as a stand-in father for help and guidance, but as a polygamous man, he looked at her—his own flesh-and-blood niece—as a potential wife, and tried to seduce her. "I have to get out of here now," Becky said when she told us what happened.

My cousin Aaron Wayman and my brother-in-law Danny Allred were working on a job for Phaze Concrete in Pagosa Springs, Colorado, just then, and they asked me to bring the children for a visit, so Becky and I decided to take our kids and check it out that very night. It was a ten-hour drive through a storm, but we made it to Colorado Springs in one piece. Aaron had gotten us a hotel suite with two bedrooms where we could stay until we decided what to do.

Aaron had rented a house with a hot tub on the porch, and we were over there every day. Sitting in that tub with my kids as the snow fell around us was like a cozy dream. We swam at the hot springs every day too. Swimsuits were still too revealing for us, so we made happily do with short pants and T-shirts.

"I'm considering calling David," Becky said after we put the children to bed one night. She hadn't seen her husband since Father had sent him away forever in 2012. He'd been living alone in Salt Lake City ever since.

"You should," I said. "At least give him a chance."

Becky phoned him right then, and I went to bed. During the night, I got up a few times to check on her, but she was still on the phone. We didn't talk until morning.

"He's coming up here to get me," Becky said.

"Seriously?"

"We talked about everything, and he said he wants us with him."

I was really happy for Becky, that she would get to be with the man she loved and the father of her children after struggling for so long. But I was a little unnerved as well. I was on my own now.

26

Answered Prayers

I wasn't going back to Centennial, that was for sure. I loved my relatives there, and I was very grateful for their help, but I didn't like the way so many men there were on the lookout for more wives. It seemed so unfair to the wives they already had.

Becky was moving to Salt Lake City with her husband, and I'd grown up on the outskirts in Sandy, so I thought I'd go there too. I knew my brother Roy was already there; he was the oldest child of Father's third wife, Gloria Barlow. Father had never treated him very well, and he had left the church a year earlier. I didn't have a number or address for him, but I found him through Facebook.

Roy told me about an organization called Holding Out HELP, a nonprofit group that provides resources to people leaving the FLDS—everything from personal hygiene products to clothes to doctors and attorneys and housing placement. I met with Tanya Tewill, the group's founder, and she put me in touch with an older couple who offered me two rooms in their house until another house could be found. The couple were very kind to us, but it was difficult staying in someone else's house with five children who weren't in school because we didn't know where we'd be living long-term.

One of the first things I did while I came up with a plan was change my older daughters' names. I had never liked the names Father had given them, and neither did they. Barbie became Ember Rose, and Martha became Majasa Gold. An attorney named Roger Hoole did the legal paperwork for us pro bono.

We'd been in Salt Lake just a few days when my cousin Aaron Wayman called and asked if we'd like to come live with him in Amarillo, Texas, where he'd recently moved for Phaze Concrete. Aaron was now a foreman and made a good income, so he kept working there, even though in his heart he, too, had left the church.

"If you find a house before Holding Out HELP does, then we will move in with you," I told him.

Within a week, Aaron had found a small house in the middle of town with a brown fence around the backyard. We didn't mind that it was small, since it was temporary. (Aaron had plans to move to Montana when he'd saved up enough money in any case.) I liked that idea, too, because I loved the mountains. In the meantime, he borrowed a trailer to hitch to his truck, and came to get us for the drive to Texas.

Aaron introduced my children to activities they'd never been allowed to do in the church. The first time we went skiing was a revelation. Majasa, brave and wild, took to the slopes like a pro. Rulon, only seven years old, was also a quick learner and conquered the big trails in no time. Ember and I weren't so brave, and my first run down the beginning slope was a mess. *This is supposed to be fun?* But by my third run, I started to get the hang of it and enjoy myself. The real prize for me was the joy in my heart at seeing my children having fun.

It was spring by then—tornado season in that part of the country—and we did see some fierce storms and heard plenty of tornado warnings, but we never did experience a twister, which was fine by me.

Several times after I left, I asked my Uncle Isaac if I could speak to Rich. He told me that Rich had chosen to obey Father, so he would not talk to me.

I had to face that Rich wanted to live in the church, under Father's harsh rules, but I couldn't understand how he could make no effort to find his children, or speak to them, or even inquire if they were okay. It was hard for the children to accept that their father cared more about the church than about them. I don't believe a reasonable man would let someone else get between him and his own family, but Rich had allowed Father to do exactly that.

We'd been staying with Aaron in Amarillo a couple of months when his bosses at Phaze Concrete found out he had us apostates living with him and fired him. Rather than being a bad thing, it freed us up sooner than expected, and we all moved to Polson, Montana, in early June.

We found a ranch on twenty acres of land there. The house was a cozy three-bedroom with a loft. The only challenge was all of us having to share a single bathroom, but we managed. In August I enrolled my children in a small country public school called Valley View. The children had an easier time adjusting there than they'd had at the larger public school they'd attended in Centennial. The schoolhouse had only two classrooms, one for kindergarten through grade three, and the other for grades four to six. There was a nice playground surrounded by fields of potatoes, corn, and wheat. The children loved it when they saw cowboys moving herds of cows down the road that passed in front of the school.

I decided to focus on my education now too. Since I had stopped attending our church school after eighth grade, I had a lot of catching up to do, but I managed to get my GED in a month and then started to take classes at SKC College in Ronan. It was sometimes difficult helping the children with their homework and getting my own homework done, but we did it. I gave violin lessons when I wasn't in school.

I worried that I wasn't being a good mom when I spent my energy trying to get good grades of my own, and at times I felt overwhelmed and alone, but I was determined to provide for my kids. The church had not prepared me to work in the outside world, to make a living to support my family. It didn't prepare any of the women to do that. All we could do was sew and cook and clean. The men at least had skills in useful trades, like construction or furniture making. The only way I was going to get a good job was to get an education. I also continued giving violin lessons for an income.

My brother Ray found me on Facebook not long after we got to Montana to tell me he was leaving too. I talked to Aaron about it, and agreed that Ray could move in with us. He didn't live with us very long, because he was quickly able to get a place of his own—who can blame him, what with the one bathroom and all those kids?—but he helped us out a lot.

After the last time I saw him in Short Creek, Ray had moved in with Rich, and he asked him about what I'd told him. Rich acknowledged that Father had confessed, but "Rachel isn't supposed to talk about that." When Father found out that Ray had asked, he sent Ray away from our family to work for Phaze, which only confirmed that what I'd told him was true. Ray was just twenty-one years old when he decided to get out.

I hadn't seen my husband in four years, but it was hard to let him go and think of myself as single.

I was thirty-one years old, and I had no idea how to date; it was a scary prospect. With five children, too, it seemed nearly impossible. When we were still in Salt Lake, I guess word got out that Warren Jeffs's daughter was available, and men did contact me, asking to go out with me, but I turned them all down. Some of the older men already had wives, and the younger men who had no families were no match for a woman with five kids. Perhaps I was too picky, but I had enough on my plate as it was.

I still felt that way when we moved to Montana, not far from another FLDS outpost just across the border in Canada, which meant there were other former church members in the area. A man in Canada who had left the church a few years earlier reached out and asked if I would let him court me, but he already had two wives, so I politely told him I wasn't going to live in polygamy again.

"Would you be willing to talk to my brother?" the man said. "He doesn't believe in polygamy either."

I agreed to talk to the man's brother, but fully expected nothing to come of it.

That brother was Brandon. He and I started talking casually at first. Brandon was a little less than a year older than me, and had been married in the church also, but he had left in 2012. His ex-wife, whom Father had chosen for him, was still in the church, and she and Brandon shared custody of their four children.

Brandon and I met for the first time a few weeks later, near the end of October 2015. We decided to meet in the Walmart parking lot in Kalispell, then he would drive us in his truck to Glacier National Park. I got there first and waited, my nerves growing more jangly with each passing minute that he was late. He finally pulled up next to me and rolled down his window.

"Hi," Brandon said. He was wearing sunglasses, so I couldn't tell what his eyes looked like, but I didn't dare ask him to remove them. He quickly explained he didn't have a GPS in his truck, so it had taken him a little while to find the place, since he'd never been there before.

On the way to the park, we talked and got to know each other. Brandon seemed very genuine, and I found it easy to confide in him. We went to dinner at Applebee's that evening. As we sat down at our table, he finally took off his shades, and I was struck by how handsome he was. But it was how kind and caring he was that really got to me. I think we were both too nervous to eat much. Brandon had to get back for work, so he took me back to my car after dinner before heading back to Canada. I so wanted him to hug me, but I don't think either of us dared. This was new territory for us both. It was new and exciting to spend time with someone because I chose to.

On our second date, we met in Bonner's Ferry. That time, we hugged.

Together, we planned a trip to Southern California at the end of the year. We had a friend, Marty, who had left the FLDS and become a Navy SEAL. He was stationed in San Diego, and he'd invited us to stay with him. My brother Ray and sister Angela came too.

The four of us arrived in the evening, and we all stayed up late talking and laughing with Marty and his wife until we cried. The next morning, we visited the Fort Rosecrans National Cemetery. I had never seen anything like it, the rows and rows of identical stones commemorating fallen members of the military, set against a panoramic view of the bay. I was filled with a sense of reflection and peace.

Later that day we put on our swimsuits, and Marty took us to the Coronado beach where the SEALs train. We spent the afternoon in the ocean, my first visit since that brief experience in Galveston when I visited Father in prison. The salty sweetness of the ocean made me incredibly happy, and I wanted to soak up every moment of it. I walked all the way out until the water came up to my shoulders, diving under the waves as they came toward me. Brandon worried I was too far out and asked me to come back, but I stayed right where I was. I was fine.

As the sun was sinking toward the western horizon, Brandon said, "We need to get a sunset picture up on the tower at the obstacle course." So Marty and his wife, Angela and Ray, and Brandon and I all jumped into Marty's ride and drove over to the course where the SEALs trained. Brandon and Marty lifted me up onto the tower, which they called the "high slide for life," and Brandon climbed up after me, followed by Marty, to take our picture. I could see a storm brewing in the distance, which made the sunset even more spectacular, the waves crashing along the shore below. I was mesmerized by the view.

Suddenly, Brandon dropped to one knee in front of me. "Rachel, will you marry me?"

I was stunned. No one had ever proposed to me before. This was all so new for me, I didn't know what I was doing or how to respond. I said, "Yes."

Brandon placed a ring on my finger and stood up so Marty could take our picture. He teased us and made us laugh. They lowered me down to the beach, where Marty performed a mock wedding for us.

"Do you, brother Brandon, take sister Rachel by the right hand and marry her to yourself?" he said.

Brandon laughed and said yes.

"Dear sister Rachel, do you take this dear brother Brandon by the right hand and give yourself to him?"

I was laughing too. "Yup," I said.

"Then, dear brother Brandon, you may kiss her."

Brandon put his strong arms around me, and we kissed there with the sand between our toes, the waves of the ocean lapping at the shore, and a lovely sunset behind us.

It was a day I marked as "very happy" in my life. It was wonderful to choose a man, to fall in love naturally, instead of having my life arranged by Father. I felt so free and full of love I could hardly place my happiness.

I moved into my own house with my kids in January 2016. It was an older house, but big, with five bedrooms, a large living space downstairs, and lots of windows that let the light in. It felt good to be on my own finally, although it was difficult making ends meet. Oftentimes I wondered if I'd be able to manage, but somehow things worked out, and Brandon helped us a lot. Then my landlord got engaged and decided he needed my house for himself. He gave me less than a month's notice to find a new place.

I didn't have a credit history or a regular job, so it was hard to find a house we could afford. Brandon helped me look from Salt Lake City up to the Canadian border, but nothing looked promising. I cried and prayed a lot during the month of May as the June deadline approached. We both applied for a number of places, but never heard back from the real estate agents.

Then, just nine days before we were going to be evicted and I was running out of hope, a man called from Idaho. "I don't care about credit or anything like that. Just give me your landlord's number, and if he gives a good payment history, you can rent my home."

The relief I felt was indescribable. We moved to Idaho a few days later. After all this time, it seemed my prayers had finally been answered.

Epilogue

Life never ends up the way I think it's going to. It surprises me in so many ways every day, some good, some bad. Being grateful for whatever life hands me is the key to my sanity and happiness.

I will always be grateful for my time with Rich. He made me feel like a good person. He made me feel loved and showed me that all men are not like my father. Because of him, I learned to compose music, make cheese, milk cows, and drive a tractor. Rich made me laugh, shared beautiful sunsets with me, and gave me five precious gifts in my children. I wish I had told him how I really felt the last time I saw him, that I had disobeyed the rules and hugged and kissed him and told him I loved him. I have to remind myself often that it wouldn't have changed anything: he isn't here now, he doesn't help take care of his children, and I don't feel the same way toward him now.

It has not been easy adjusting to life in the outside world, learning to navigate a whole new way of living, and supporting five children as a single mother has been a struggle, but having our freedom is worth it. I love that we can go play dodgeball on the trampoline or lie out under the stars and tell scary stories. In the summer we swim, pick huckleberries, and go hiking. In the winter we go tubing down our hills, ice skating at the park, or jump off the roof of the garage into the enormous piles of snow that comes down here.

"Come on, Mom! Come dance with us!" That's what my kids

say to me almost every evening now as one of them takes my arm and leads me into the living room.

"I'll run the music," Majasa says. She's a pro at finding the best tunes for us to jam out to. The girls, young teenagers now, do one-handed cartwheels and try to teach me the latest dance steps, moves from jazz to hip-hop to ballet. We love it all. The boys have their own tricks to show off. Rulon flies around the room doing flips and cartwheels and twirls on his head, and his little brother tries to copy his moves. Seven-year-old Nathaniel is determined to teach me how to do a cartwheel. "It takes a lot of tries before you can do it good," he tells me. I try to do one for his sake, but I can't seem to get my legs up in the air. "It's okay, Mom, you're good at lots of other things." I laugh, and we keep boogying, tumbling, and laughing our faces off. Our evening dance time is silly and joyful and by far our favorite part of the day. I believe God loves to see us enjoy life with our families.

I still have bad dreams about Father. In some of these dreams, Father insists that I have sex with him every night, and there is nowhere for me to escape. During the day, I gather my little sisters to protect them from him. I tell my sisters to make sure to lock their doors at night. As night falls, I am overwhelmed with dread of what I know is to come.

In some of these dreams, Father grips my wrist tightly and explains to me why God wants me to have a baby with him. He won't let go until I promise to have a baby with him.

In some of these dreams, I hear Father telling my little sisters why God wants them to have sex with him. I step in and tell him to do it to me instead, since he has already hurt me. I don't want them to suffer as I have.

I hate how these dreams still plague me. I hope with all my

heart and soul that someday they will go away. But I know that I am fortunate, because these are just dreams. For many of his family, the nightmare is still all too real.

In late August 2016 Father sent letters from prison in which he said that his family was unworthy of him and that God would give him a new family. He sent seven of his most special wives away forever with instructions that they must leave their children behind. This edict, like so many others that have come from behind those prison walls, hurts my heart. Father has trained his family, especially the women, in such a way that they cannot survive outside the church.

Father's twelve-year-old bride Alysha, now twenty-four, who was living with us in hiding in Idaho, recently escaped with the man she always loved. She came to visit me and asked to hear my story. After I finished telling her, she said, "Rachel, why didn't you tell us sooner so we didn't have to waste all those years there?"

I smiled and said, "You wouldn't have believed me."

"You're right," she said. "Sometimes we have to go through hell ourselves before we are humble enough to listen."

She then told me that Father sent a message to all of his family after we, his daughters, left the church, saying the reason we left is because we were guilty of masturbating and would not confess to him. (I can just imagine the image my brothers and sisters have of me.)

We are all taught that leaving the church is the greatest sin, and that anyone who does is wicked. A number of people who left the church before me reached out to hear my story. After I'd repeated it several times, I started to write it down. My father's wives are lost without the church, but they will not speak to me because they still believe that I am wicked.

I hope they will come to believe that what they've been taught is a lie, that the world is not a wicked place, and that they are worthy of God's love.

To all my family still in the church, or cast out but afraid to reach out, you always have a home at my house.

Until then, I pray.

Family Tree

WARREN JEFFS

78 Wives
53 Children

Annette Barlow
  Maryanne Jeffs
  Sandra Jeffs
  Becky Jeffs
  Shirley Jeffs
  Angela Jeffs
  Mosiah Jeffs
  Teresa Jeffs
  Helaman Jeffs
  Hannah Jeffs
  Abraham Jeffs
  Suzie Jeffs
  William Jeffs
Barbara Barlow
(Annette's sister)
  Rachel Jeffs
  Melanie Jeffs
  Levi Jeffs
  Ammon Jeffs
  Josephine Jeffs
  Jacob Jeffs
  Joseph Jeffs
  Amber Jeffs
Gloria Barlow
  Leroy Jeffs

  Richard Jeffs
  Patricia Jeffs
  Rulon Jeffs
Brenda Jessop
  Raymond Jeffs
  Isaac Jeffs
Monica Jessop
  Barbara Jeffs
  Nephi Jeffs
  SweetMarie Jeffs
  Naomi Jeffs
  Monica Sue Jeffs
Sharon Barlow
  Samuel Jeffs
Shannon Johnson
  Kendra Jeffs
  Kendall Jeffs
  Seth Jeffs
  Maria Jeffs
Vicki Nielsen
  Wendell Jeffs
  Sarah Jeffs
Jessica Johnson
Nicole Blackmore

Lana Blackmore
Lori Steed
   Elizabeth Jeffs
Amy Draper
Mildred Jessop
   Milly Jeffs
   Merril Jeffs
   Johnathon Jeffs
Jennifer Steed
   Melissa Jeffs
   Shem Jeffs
Joanna Steed
   Heaven Sent Jeffs
Sheena Roundy
Margaret Jessop
Sharon Steed
Rebekah Seed
Clea Steed
Bonnie Lee Black
Ada Johnson
Ida Mae Johnson
Ida Lorraine Jessop
Alice Barlow
Ora Steed
   Rulon W. Jeffs
   Nettie Jeffs
   Mormon Jeffs
Naomi Jessop
Patricia Keate
   Kathryn Jeffs
   Mahonri Jeffs
Melinda Johnson
Tammy Steed
Paula Jessop
Kathy Blackmore
Kate Jessop
Velvet Jessop
   Velvet Rose Jeffs
Lorraine Roundy

Asenath Jessop
Gladys Jessop
Shanna Zitting
Fern Steed
Maria Jessop
Ruthie Jessop
   Michelle Jeffs
Debbie Barlow
Veda Keate
   Serena Jeffs
Esther Barlow
Lynette Warner
Gloria Anne Steed
Annie Jessop
Michelle Barlow
Ida Vilate
Marianne Jessop
Lorretta Barlow
Colleen Warner
Brenda Lee Fisher
Gloria Roundy
Carla Jessop
Stella Jessop
Esther Jessop
Joanne Barlow
Winnie Steed
Anna Mae Blackmore
Alysha Blackmore
Colleen Blackmore
Marleen Blackmore
Tamara Allred
Susan Harker
Permelia Johnson
Angela Barlow
Roberta Steed
Jennetta Jessop
Lisa Steed

Jennifer Wall
Carneta Holm
Shirley Steed
Mary Fisher
Caroline Nielson
Shauna Jessop
Nancy Steed

Children in age order:
  Maryanne
  Sandra
  Rachel
  Becky
  Melanie
  Shirley
  Angela
  Levi
  Mosiah
  Ammon
  Teresa
  Leroy
  Josephine
  Helaman
  Raymond
  Richard
  Hannah
  Isaac
  Patricia
  Barbara
  Abraham
  Jacob

Nephi
Rulon
Kendra
Suzie
Joseph
Kendall
SweetMarie
Wendell
Milly
Melissa
Amber
Elizabeth
William
Naomi
Samuel
Heaven
Sarah
Kathryn
Rulon Warren
Nettie
Merril
Seth
Shem
Monica
Michelle
Maria
Serena
Mormon
Johnathon
Mahonri
Velvet

Acknowledgments

I want to give special thanks to the following people:

My sisters Angela and Becky and my brother Ray, for always being there for me no matter what Father said.

My grandpa Isaac's family, for giving us a place to live when we left.

My cousin Aaron Wayman and brother-in-law Danny Allred, for helping support us when we first left.

Brandon, for your love and support.

Tawni Browning, for helping me in so many ways.

Rose Dutson and Annie Blackmore, for being my friends.

At HarperCollins, my editor, Luke Dempsey, and publisher, Jonathan Burnham.

My agent, Heather Jackson, at the David Black Literary Agency.

Elizabeth Stein, for her help writing the book.

I was not present at my Father's trials or the raid at the land of refuge in Texas, so I relied in part on reporting in the *New York Times*, the *Deseret News*, and especially the excellent in-depth reporting by Katy Vine in *Texas Monthly* for some dates and facts about those events. Additionally, I also referred to my sister Teresa's book, *2008 Raid*. Upon learning of its publication, Father promptly sent her a strong correction telling her that Heavenly Father was displeased with her for making her story public and instructing her to burn all ten copies she had made. At her request, I burned the copy she had given me. However, she also asked me to keep an electronic copy, for which I am very grateful.

About the Author

Rachel Jeffs grew up in the Fundamentalist Church of Jesus Christ of Latter-Day Saints, the polygamous Mormon sect, which she escaped in 2015. Rachel and her five children live in Idaho.